NETWORK MARKETING ONLINE

THE ONLY TESTED SYSTEM ABLE TO RECRUIT 700 PEOPLE IN 9 MONTHS BY DOING MULTILEVEL MARKETING - MLM - ON SOCIAL MEDIA

(ESPECIALLY FOR FACEBOOK AND INSTAGRAM)

DREAMWORKERS TEAM

Copyright © 2019 by Dreamworkers Team

All rights reserved. No part of this book may be used or reproduced by any means, graphic, electronic, or mechanical, including photocopying, recording, taping, or by any information storage retrieval system, without the written permission of the publisher except in the case of brief quotations embodied in critical articles and reviews.

LEGAL DISCLAIMER

The authors and the publisher have made every effort to ensure the accuracy of the information contained in this book at the time of publication.

The authors and the publisher therefore do not assume, and hereby disclaim any liability, to any party for any loss, damage or interruption caused by errors or omissions, whether such errors or omissions arise from accident, negligence or any other cause.

The information contained in this book is for educational purposes only. If you apply the ideas contained in the book, you assume full responsibility for your actions, and there is no guarantee of duplicating the results indicated here.

Each individual's success is determined by their desire, effort, knowledge and motivation to work in their company.

SPECIAL OFFER

As a special thank you for purchasing this book, I have prepared an exclusive gift for you.

Now you can join the DreamWorkers Team and receive the most advanced program in Italy on Network Marketing, **DREAMWORKERS ACCELERATOR**, for free instead of 1.997€.

Click on the following link to watch our presentation and reserve a 30-minute strategic counseling session with one of our coaches.

=> https://bit.ly/dwtexpansion <=

Follow us on our Facebook Page:

=> https://www.facebook.com/dreamworkersteam/

Table of Contents

Introduction 1

Chapter 1: How To Structure A Winning Mindset 14

Chapter 2: Identify The Correct Market Niche 59

Chapter 3: Package Offer 88

Chapter 4: Anatomy Of A Marketing Ecosystem 99

Chapter 5: Sources Of Traffic 112

Chapter 6: Scripts To Use For The Call 135

Chapter 7: Set A Correct Followup 150

Conclusion 164

Strategic Ps: The Real Problem With The Funnels 168

INTRODUCTION

Before starting any speech, I want to congratulate you because the decision to buy this book is definitely one of the most important.

Over 95% of networkers do not earn a single euro throughout their careers because they try to carry out this activity without knowing how to do it and with what tools.

In the collective imagination, anyone can do network marketing.

This way of thinking has totally destroyed the category, leading it rightly to be perceived as a niche of people who tried everything and, as a last resort, embark on an extreme attempt.

For this reason, if you are here and you are reading these words, you will have on your side the odds, which will lead you to be included in that 5% that creates a solid business and capable of generating income.

Network Marketing Online

One of the main things you need to understand is that network marketing does not exist: network marketing is doing marketing within a network, that is selling something to a certain niche of people on which you have influence.

It is much more likely that you are doing, instead, multilevel marketing, as your goal is to sell products, services or directly the business opportunity and then teach the lower levels to do the same thing.

If you understand this, you also understand the importance of marketing, which will help you bring the right offer to the right people through the right marketing ecosystem that can then convert them.

That's where the problem of the name list comes from: your sponsor or your up-line told you to write down a certain number of contacts (from the hottest, which would give you the credit card without even knowing what you're talking about, to the coldest) and contact them as tricky to bring them to a presentation.

If you analyzed your contacts before calling them, you would realize that 99% of these people are not at all in target, that is, they are not able to carry out your project.

The reason for this is very simple and will be examined in detail when we talk about how to structure the right offer.

You are going to offer them a product or service to sell without a marketing ecosystem to do so (the name list is not a marketing ecosystem) and the new subscriber will then have to contact friends to stick this stuff to them in exchange for two pennies.

By duplicating this process, you realize how easy it is to destroy the reputation of an entire market segment.

When people look at network marketing and networkers with disgust today, I am not surprised, but reluctantly I'm forced to agree with them.

The reason they teach people to make lists is because they need to reach as many people as possible by making them believe that it is simple and that everyone can do it, when in fact the statistics show us exactly the opposite.

If more than 95% fail resoundingly, then there is something wrong.

Then you'll wonder why some people can go on in this area with these techniques even though they are highly unsuccessful.

You should know that there are 7 very powerful unavowable desires that would lead people to do anything:

1. Greed

2. Sex

3. Make a better deal than others and belong to a small circle

4. Health

5. Self-improvement

6. Respect, revenge

7. Pleasure, fun

Desire number 6 is the one on which highly successful networkers have built empires and worldwide networks. I'll tell you why.

The main target of these networkers, as I've just told you, is represented by a whole series of people who no longer know where to bang their heads, who have serious economic problems, who have major social difficulties, who have a low level of self-esteem, who are unable to do anything else, who have a poor education and so on.

In simple terms, I'm not talking about the highest part of society.

That being said, once these guys have been recruited, by selling them the dream of being able to do it, they are immediately projected on the qualifications and towards the climb to success, taking their attention away from the money.

Going on stage in front of hundreds or thousands of people and telling your own success story becomes the highest aspiration, because for these people, who have never been considered by friends, relatives and maybe even by their parents, getting revenge and respect becomes a matter of fundamental importance.

Just bring them on stage for the first time, make them smell the scent of success, and trap them forever within a mechanism from which they will hardly get out.

At that precise moment they would do anything to maintain their qualifications or stay within this business, because the opposite would mean to agree with all the people who had little consideration of them.

So, at the cost of investing much more than they earn, they continue to push like there was no tomorrow to keep the rank or jump to the next one and remain the best in the eyes of many.

On the other hand there are the big fish, also known as sharks, that motivate them with a pat on the back and make them feel like successful people, in order to make this game even more perverse.

These people begin to get respect not only from friends, but also from successful people and, if you consider that the day before they were nobody, you can understand the strength of this mechanism.

That's why, when they say the list of names works, it's actually true. Too bad it only works for that tiny percentage of sharks ready to devour any smaller fish and it works thanks to a perverse mechanism from which I prefer to stay away.

If you think about it and look at your own downline or the downlines of other networkers, maybe even of other companies, who are the so-called diamonds?

They are people who have a certain influence on a specific niche market and who manage, in a short time, to enrol a lot of people because they are respected and considered successful.

The main goal of the list of names is to annihilate hundreds of them to get to the next diamond, which will annihilate even more until you find another one and so on.

Network Marketing Online

A weapon of mass destruction which, through the manipulation of people's decision-making processes and dreams, makes its way into the crowd until the next big fish is caught.

Let's say it's a sad story and a mediocre way to run a business. That's why in this book I'm going to try to transfer a more articulated strategy to you, which will allow you to have in your team people who are aware of what they're going against.

And keep in mind that this stuff is not surpassed by creating an online system, because even there you can just recruit the poor guy on duty to sell a dream that will never come true and, if you are good, you will do even more damage because you will reach more people in a shorter time.

So, working online is fine, but you have to build a system that will remove all the people who are not in the target, who do not have entrepreneurial vision.

Dreamworkers Team

The aim of this book is to give you a mechanism capable of making you talk every day only with interested people, who want to study, grow and invest.

If you aim for tomorrow's success and not for the long term one, your network marketing activity will never be solid and will never make you sleep peacefully.

One piece of advice I want to give you is to devote a lot of attention to everything you read, especially the first two chapters, even if they are the heaviest.

They are the ones that will give you the chance to bring your people in charge to success and create real success stories, stories of people who earn money, not medals.

In addition, click on the following link to see how the recruitment system I use is built, so that you can compare the study with reality.

=> https://bit.ly/dwtexpansion

Always remember that real money come when you help people, not when you pretend to.

The better your downline results, the more people will bring home some profit and the more likely you are to scale this business.

The first chapter is about the mindset and everything you have to do to be part of those very few successful people who succeed in everything they undertake.

The second chapter will show you in detail how to identify a profitable market niche to show your offer, which you will learn to build impeccably thanks to the third chapter.

In the fourth we will build our marketing ecosystem capable of qualifying in the best possible way all the people who will eventually come to talk to us.

We will talk about sources of organic and paid traffic in the fifth chapter and we will get to the sixth that will show you the exact script to use in call to have a high conversion rate.

After that there will be the last chapter, before the conclusion, where I will attach some followup emails I use for my mailing list.

But before you begin, I will tell you who I am and why you should read every word of this book very carefully, until the end.

My name is Matteo and I founded the DreamWorkers Team on March 3, 2018.

This was my first experience in network marketing, even if I come from a similar industry, that is marketing.

I used to and still sell high ticket info-products in different market niches and I advise entrepreneurs who work online or who simply have real activities to grow nationally or internationally.

I started with network marketing totally by mistake and, I dare say, like any other person.

One day one of my clients invited me to discuss a project and I became, on that same day, the subject of the presentation of a product he had just begun to promote by working with the company with which I work at this time.

Network Marketing Online

At first, my idea was to use the service without entering the business, but, given my propensity to monetize anything that passes me by, the decision to add this new asset to my portfolio was not slow to arrive.

If we add to this the very low, not to say irrelevant, competition in the sector the company has for growth and size, I would say that I made a more than optimal choice.

In the first year of activity I created a network of almost a thousand people and I began to notice the first difficulties of duplication, which resulted from the lack of after-sales training and many other difficulties that each person had in proposing this business opportunity.

That's why I decided to lock myself up at home for a couple of months and pull out a duplicable system that would allow anyone to get huge advantages over any other competitor, whether from the same company or not.

A system that allowed me to invest time and energy only in the generation of contacts, forgetting everything that comes after, thanks to a team dedicated to customer service and continuous training of the entire network.

If you consider that almost no one in the world can duplicate a solid sales system to the entire downline, you immediately understand the potential that you have in your hands now you have made the decision to read this book.

I certainly do not claim to turn you into the strongest networker in history, but I can reasonably say I am putting in your hands something that has led me and the other people in my team to achieve amazing results by working with absolutely in target people.

So, we just have to start...

CHAPTER 1

HOW TO STRUCTURE A WINNING MINDSET

In this first chapter you'll find out what 99% of people who fail in every aspect of their lives are missing.

People fail not only when they start a business, but also when they start a diet, decide to play sports, try to win over a girl and in everything else they try to do.

They fail because there is a problem with their mindset, related to a whole series of paradigms installed inside their brain, which lead them to perform unsuccessful actions.

You can be profitable with your business only after replacing these patterns with successful ones belonging to 1% of the population.

You have to know that the majority of people fail in everything they do, not because they lack the action or do not have the correct techniques, rather they lack an adequate mindset.

If you devote less focus to these concepts to spend most of your time mastering the best technique, failure will be just around the corner.

You will be inclined to skip this part to get straight to the strategy, but I advise you not to do so, because here you will find the most important elements and everything else will be simply something technical that you have to adapt to your reality.

If you need it, read this chapter over and over again, because if you build your business a week later, nobody will die, but if you do it without the correct mindset you will simply die.

You have lived quietly until today, for better or for worse, and a few days will not change your life.

The time you invest from this precise moment onwards will bring you the greatest return on your investment and will forever detach you from your competitors.

If you are in a hurry to launch your business without working on your mindset, you will not build something solid and you will need, at a later time, more time to improve other aspects, because your business will be watering down everywhere.

And I can guarantee that.

What will you find in this chapter?

We will start from the objective, we will understand what is the real objective that you have to reach and how to identify it, if you do not have it clear inside your brain, how to structure it and how to achieved it.

At this point, you will be aware that what you are doing right now is not correct.

If there is a gap between what should be your goal, your point of arrival, and what is your current situation, it is because there are actions that you are doing every day that will not lead you to the achievement of that goal.

So, being aware of this is another step further, which will give you the opportunity to work on your mindset.

We will see how we can be focused every day to accomplish our objective, carrying out actions that are congruent and in line with the path that we are going to build.

We will see how important it is to do massive action every day, how to do it and how to be absolutely focused on one and the same goal.

This is because when we structure the entire business, so that our energy is all focused on one and the same point, we will have the strength to bring this business to be duplicable and scalable.

When our energies disperse, they go left and right, because we do not have a clear point, we do not have a small point on which we go to unleash all hell, we do not have the opportunity to make the business profitable.

We will also see how wrong it is to be a perfectionist and try to have the best system to bring to market.

So, once again, pay a lot of attention to this chapter.

Network Marketing Online

Read it 10,000 times and spend as much time as you can on it, because it is the most important part and the biggest stone in the foundations of the skyscraper you are going to build.

If you are here reading this book, it is definitely not to reach a monetary target.

I know that all you are doing is to reach a monetary target, but actually that monetary target is needed to reach another target that is the most important: the monetary target is simply the means to reach your ultimate goal.

Your task at this precise moment is to dig deep and understand exactly what the real goal is, that is, why you need material means.

Above all, if you have a target in monetary terms and already know what is the amount you want to achieve, the question to ask yourself is why?

The question is, what are you going to use that for?

If you do not understand that your goal is not monetary and that you only need money to achieve it, you will not be able to work on your mindset and to install the correct paradigms that will lead you to be part of 1%.

To do this, you need to ask yourself some questions.

First of all, what's wrong with you?

What hurts you?

Why can't you be happy and quiet and live the life you have always wanted?

What is the GAP between your ideal situation and the current one? What is missing?

What do you need to wake up in the morning with a smile?

Maybe you want to win over a girl, or maybe you have a mortgage to pay, so you need the money to pay it off and live a quiet life.

In this case, your goal is not to become a millionaire, but simply to live a relaxed life.

Maybe you want to continue doing what you have always done, because you like your work and you are satisfied with it. But you are not doing it the right way, because your earnings are enough to survive, not to pay the mortgage of your house.

Maybe you earnings are enough for you to live, but you are terrified every day because there may be redundancies in your factory, office, or wherever you are working, in a few years.

So you say "okay what I am fine with what I am doing now, that's enough, but every day I live with the paranoia that tomorrow something might happen that will lead me to not be able to move forward".

And so, once again, your goal of making money is always a goal related to peace, to live peacefully, maybe with your wife and your children.

Once you know this, you also manage to structure your mind correctly to achieve that goal and you also manage to have a monthly turnover target totally different from the simple "I need tot", because you know that you need tot in tot time, so all your actions will be carried out in a totally different way.

Understand exactly what is the gap between what is the ideal life objective and what you are living at the moment is essential to understand how much you actually need to fill this gap.

When you know exactly what is missing between your current level and your ideal level, you have to quantify a figure you need each month to live the life you have always wanted.

Maybe today you are earning 2000€ a month and you need 1500€ more a month to live your desired lifestyle.

All the actions that we have to carry out implementing this business must be focused on reaching those 1500€ per month.

When you have a precise monthly economic monetary target, you will be able to structure your business; you will be able to set everything I teach you in this book correctly to achieve that target.

Other questions to ask are...

How long are you willing to sacrifice?

How willing are you to work hard?

How many years of defeats, failures and people mocking are you willing to face?

How ready are you to complicate and worsen your current situation?

I know that everyone looking for other people to join the team or trying to sell a system to generate income online or offline, says that it is simple.

I know that we all have the image of the boy on the beach with a cocktail in his hand and a bank account slowly growing; I know that everyone believes in automatic systems and Ponzi schemes.

The problem is that the 1% that makes big money gets its ass kicked all the time and much more than everyone else.

This is the only truth. So, if the result you have now comes from a whole series of actions you are doing every day, the only way to vary that result is to change your actions. To achieve a different result, you not only need different actions, but you also need to make your life more complicated and learn to do things that you are not able to do today.

When you are able to do different things, those different actions will give you a totally different result. But you can never have a different result if you continue living the life you have always lived.

If your life is simple, if you wake up every day despite your problems, despite the gap between your future goal and your current situation, if there is no complication, if there are no problems to face and there are no flaps, most likely you are not working properly to achieve your real goal.

If you are at a totally different level from the level that can take you to your goal, you need to make your life more complicated. You need to make a quality leap and to move from the current level to the next level, bringing in a whole series of problems, problems that will later become simple stuff that will fill your coffers.

Every time you implement something new into your life, that something new creates problems.

Therefore, you need to be able to solve that problem right away.

The larger the gap between your future goal and your current situation, the more problems you have to introduce into your life, the more you have to be willing to sacrifice your life and work hard.

The awareness of everything I have said so far, that you are not able to achieve what is your real goal because you are putting in place different actions, comes from the simple fact that everything is measured in relation to its results.

Dreamworkers Team

If you do not have the lifestyle you desire, everything you are thinking right now doesn't matter and it doesn't matter to anyone; and if someone cares, that someone doesn't matter.

This is something you absolutely need to install inside your brain.

There is no such thing as "I think", "They told me", "They advised me" or "They told me".

There is only one result!

If there is a gap between your hoped-for situation and your current one and if you are not able to fill that gap right now, it is because everything you think, everything people around you think is totally wrong.

This is something objective that cannot be questioned.

No way.

Network Marketing Online

A person who earns €10,000 a month can teach me how to carry out a series of actions that can lead me to earn €10,000 a month.

If a person earns 1000€ he can't think about what he should implement to earn 10.000€ because he doesn't earn them. So it remains a thought that doesn't matter to anyone and it is not functional to the achievement of the goal, because only results matter.

If you get a result, fine. If you do not get a result, what you are doing is wrong.

What actions are determining your current results?

You currently have a result. Whether you like it or not you have a result. What you should do is to ask yourself what every day actions are leading you to that result.

When you deeply know 70%-80% of your life, when you know how you live it, what work you are doing, what are your routines, what are your actions, what are your thoughts, you will exactly know where to intervene.

Dreamworkers Team

If you write down a list of the actions you perform every day, you will know the 70%-80% of those actions that are determining your current result and you will automatically know where to act aggressively with respect to everything else.

At the same time you have to make a list of at least 5 people you mostly hang around with and understand how often you are in contact with them.

This is because, most likely, the people you are close to at the moment get more or less your same results. If you analyze the actions these people are taking to determine their result, you will realize there are many similarities with your results and with the actions generating them.

Understanding what you have in common with them and what separates you from them gives you the opportunity to realize why you are not able to achieve a different goal.

When you say that those who go with the lame learn to limp, this is actually what you mean.

For example, if a person who earns €5000 a month lives for 2 years within millionaires, like it or not that person will grow, because he/she will be influenced by people oriented to make him think differently and he/she will be likely successful.

If you put the same person together with unsuccessful people, if he/she is really good, if he/she is really strong, if he/she has really well installed paradigms, at most he/she can continue carrying out the same results, but most likely he will not even succeed in those.

He/she will tend to go down, because we basically absorb the reality we live every day.

So, the question becomes "are you willing to totally remove from your life these five or six important people who are ruling your success? What is your result?"

Removing does not mean deleting them from your address book or telling them to go to hell. It simply means that the moment you start to change, and you will change if you want to achieve a different result, you will start to think differently and you will start to have a different awareness.

You will start to work differently, to value time differently and to do things that will gradually lead you to detach from these people. There will come a time when these people will see you as a totally different person.

They will start to say that you are changing, they will start to blame you for what is happening and for the relationships you are breaking. At that precise moment you will have to answer the question I am asking you right now.

Are you willing to remove them?

If the answer is yes, you are ready for success.

If the answer is no, you do not have the chance to make a leap forward, simply because you are too attached to your current situation.

If your dream is worth much more than what people think of you and what you do, then you are willing to remove everything.

If your dream is smaller, or if it is not really a real dream (many times we do not know our real goal, or it is not so strong to make you change completely), you already know that the business you will implement, most likely, will lead to failure.

Alternatively, it will lead you to achieve results that are more or less in line with your current results. So, being able to take on this responsibility and understanding that the day will come when you will be totally different from others and they will tell you that you are changing and destroying relationships, will help you to start a journey of change in the right way.

Having said that, we can move on...

I started the chapter by talking about focus, but then we talked about how to identify the objective, how to understand if that objective is actually real and not simply a monetary objective, which in fact is simply the means to achieve the final objective. We are realizing the actions we do every day are the actions that are bringing me a result and so I have to change the actions to achieve a different result...

... now you have to understand how to work on the focus, that is how to be focused in every moment of your life to make sure that all actions are congruent and above all are penetrating.

You have to act every day like you were a pneumatic hammer that doesn't give up an inch until it gets to the other side.

What is Focus, or rather, what is the meaning of focus within this chapter?

All your energy must be focused on one and the same point which, as far as this chapter is concerned, is your goal.

As far as the whole book is concerned, it is the system within which all potential customers will end up and then turn into real customers.

However, we will always have all our energies focused on one and the same point.

That is because when you disperse your energies you cannot be strong like when you have all your energy and all your life oriented towards one and the same point.

Your dream does not make sense until it becomes an obsession, you can make fun of yourself, but you cannot make fun of the universe.

If you are not willing to work as you have never done before, I have just told you that you will never achieve a different result.

How long will you last having the world against you every day?

How long will you be able to stand up to having your parents against you, your family against you, your friends against you, the whole system against you, all the people you love against you?

Imagine a situation where everyone calls you crazy, everyone starts to tell you that what you are doing is wrong, that you are changing, that you are destroying relationships.

As I told you before, put yourself in a situation where you understand that the rest of the world is against you.

In addition, if you want to be part of 1%, you will have 99% against you. It is just maths.

By the time you go from 99% to 1%, you will have 99% against. So, it is easier to be in the 99% because you will have no one against you, because who is part of the 1% is not even thinking about you.

How long you will last depends on the paradigms installed inside your brain.

Most likely with your current paradigms you will last very little, almost nothing. But if you change your paradigms, you will have the opportunity to hold on for longer and when you become really strong you will always hold on and be a consolidated part of that 1%.

This, of course, is not my area of expertise, all these teachings come from Bob Proctor and it is very important to understand how our mind works, how paradigms are important in achieving results.

Our mind is made up of two parts, the conscious part and the subconscious part!

Through the five senses, we influence the conscious mind. So when we eat, when we touch people, when we feel emotions, when we listen to music and hear sounds, we work on a conscious level. In short, whatever is part of the five senses influences the conscious part of our brain.

Now let's go back to target...

Which is the gap between your final goal and your current situation?

Let's pretend that it is €5,000 a month. So, on a conscious level, your goal is to achieve this amount.

The conscious mind sends the signal to the subconscious mind. When your signal arrives to the subconscious mind, all the paradigms filter the signal you are sending from the conscious mind and through this filtering, you send the signal to the body that performs actions in a specific way.

The paradigms are a whole series of elements installed inside the unconscious part of our brain, deriving from everything we constantly repeat day after day.

Again, we can say that those who go with the lame learn to limp, because if you go 365 days a year alongside a lame person you will necessarily start to limp.

This is because your unconscious is influenced by the conscious through the repetition of a certain behavior for 365 days.

When you started driving, the first time you took the wheel, everything certainly seemed difficult or almost impossible to you and you could not understand how the other people were able to drive fluently.

Surely when you took your driving lessons and the instructor told you to reverse or park, it was a drama for you.

Network Marketing Online

Today you can quietly park while listening to music, talking to someone, reading a message, because through the constant repetition of a simple action, the conscious part has managed to install into the subconscious mind something that today you can do automatically. This is a paradigm.

If you go to London, where people drive on the left, and start driving you will find it difficult because there is no paradigm, or rather the paradigm is opposite and will try to lead you to the other side.

So you need repetition to change the paradigm again.

If limiting mental paradigms about money are installed inside your unconscious mind (for example that you have to spend everything you earn, or that you don't have to have money because of the influences from the people around you), and you want to earn € 5000 per month, the paradigm will automatically make you perform actions. So, these € 5000 will find a way out as quickly as they entered and you will always stay at the starting point, ie zero.

This does not happen because you are doing things in the wrong way, but because there is an opposite paradigm that will never allow you to reach your goal.

That's why I said that this chapter is the most important, because if you don't understand that it's all a matter of paradigms, it doesn't make sense.

I mean, I can also put in your hand a system that will make you earn money, but you will not reach the goal because your paradigms are against you.

It must also be said that we are lucky if we know our paradigms.

If we do not know them, we are in a heap of trouble, because we will always do things that will never get us to the finish line, and it will be hard for us to change something we have not identified yet.

When the conscious mind sends the signal to the subconscious mind, the latter filters this signal through the paradigms.

Then it pushes out the signal, helping our bodies to work and if everything is congruent, that is, if the objective is congruent with our paradigms, we perform actions that are congruent too and lead us to achieve the objective.

Otherwise we can do everything we want, you can buy all the training courses possible and imaginable, you can open a restaurant, a pizzeria, an ice cream shop, you can do network marketing, you can do everything you want in life, you will always achieve results in line with your paradigms.

The first step to get closer to this is to buy the book "Think And Grow Rich" by Napoleon Hill (it is also available in Italian with the title "Pensa e arricchisci te stesso").

I really recommend you to read this book to start working on paradigms and actually understand how the two parts of the mind, the conscious and the subconscious one, work.

What are the patterns through which 1% of the population succeeds and 99% continues undaunted to fail?

You have to buy this book and read it as a manual over and over again.

I have read it 40 times and I am reading it again, because each sentence is capable of totally transforming your way of thinking.

The second step, which I recommend, is to watch on YouTube all Bob Proctor's videos.

The problem here is that you only find stuff in English, but this is the right time to complicate your life a bit, as we have just said, and start learning the language.

If you want to achieve the results you are not able to reach today, you have to make your life more complicated and this also means learning English.

What you have to do is study "Think And Grow Rich", which you can also find in Italian, and at the same time study Bob Proctor on YouTube videos, making these two actions a routine.

Do not study only on books, start to study also on YouTube because there you watch and listen, so you work with different senses, not just with sight.

Network Marketing Online

You have the ability to influence paradigms more strongly.

Paradigms change through repetition and a constantly repeated action gives the paradigm the possibility to change.

Paradigms are not removed, they change if they are replaced by new paradigms.

A very powerful exercise that replaces an essential paradigm for the achievement of your goals is to write at least 100 times a day this sentence:

"I'm grateful and proud now that money is coming to me in ever-increasing amounts through multiple sources and on an ongoing basis."

This is one of the sentences Bob Proctor recommends, since 1% of the population benefits continuously and systematically from more assets month after month. So, influencing the brain through repetition, writing and reading every day, gives you the opportunity to install this paradigm.

If you think this is ridiculous, you are not ready for success.

Believe it or not, my life will remain the same, I am telling you this because maybe this stuff works and I want you to achieve your goals.

Isolation is another very important element that helps to speed up the process, because it prevents the mind from being continuously flooded by garbage.

If we are surrounded every day by people with a low energy level, who are only worried about surviving, we will continue through repetition to send signals and install paradigms.

1% of the population are isolated people, people who do not communicate, people who live in a small, circumscribed reality always formed by successful people.

This does not happen because they do not want to mix with others or because they want to discredit them, simply they are not able to.

They are at a different level, they are at a different energy level.

Network Marketing Online

If you do not turn off the television and stop watching trash tv, that stuff becomes repetition that installs paradigms. If you read useless newspapers and magazines, apart from business ones, they install new files inside your brain that feed your current paradigms which produce your current results.

If you keep going bars and chatting with people saying the government steals your money, that taxes are high, that crisis is to blame, you keep installing files inside your brain.

If you're on social networks every day, if you are always on Facebook, if you are in WhatsApp groups, Telegram groups, Facebook groups, you're destroying your brain and this will destroy your life.

Isolation is the best way to speed up the process of achieving results.

So through repetition, right thoughts, YouTube videos, isolation and removal of all the crap around you, you will have a chance to achieve your goal. Then the technique will simply become the fuel on the fire, and we are lighting that fire.

Another important thing is to differentiate between caring for people and being able to help them.

When your parents tell you that you are not doing the right thing, they are actually saying it for your sake and because they love you. But if your father has been a butcher all his life and suggests you not to trade because it is risky, it is useless: even if he loves you, he cannot tell trading is risky, because he is just a butcher.

Maybe this is his opinion, but he does not have the authority to tell this. He can say he buys Kobe meat instead of a different one because that is his area of expertise, but he cannot say any more.

Understanding this is essential, because you have to accept it. You have to thank your father for loving you and trying to protect you, but you have to go doing what you have to do, even if it is not consistent with the message your father is sending you, unless you want to open a butcher shop.

Always ask yourself if the person who is talking to you is competent to do so, to that advice you.

If you need fish, go to the fish market, if you need money, go to a bank.

The problem is that people go to the fish market to ask for money and to the bank to ask for fish, you understand that it is nonsense?

Take action, study, watch videos, listen to podcasts, feed your mind every day in every possible way and you will realize that the reality you attract is a function of who you are now, of the person you are becoming.

The reason why at this precise moment you can only and attract what you have always attracted is because you are the result of all the paradigms installed in your brain.

I know it is sad, but that will make you take a real step up.

I cannot tell you that it is easy, that it is beautiful and that we all can do it, because 99% of the people who bought or will buy this book will stay at their starting point.

They will read this book and fail again, nothing strange, because after all they prefer to stay in their comfort zone rather than create a great legacy.

You are the one who has to decide to be a part of that 1%. To do this you have to reprogram your whole mind, but it is up to you to decide to reprogram it, to isolate yourself and to do everything I am trying to teach you in this chapter, it is not up on me.

I decided to do it, I decided to isolate and detach from the whole world, but I decided it by myself, I was not forced by anyone.

I am not telling you what you have to do, I am simply telling you what I have done and the results I achieved.

I read Napoleon Hill, I realized that I was not getting results because I had not programmed my mind to succeed. I reprogrammed my mind and I gradually started to be more and more successful.

The actions I was taking were correct, but the paradigms I had inside my brain were not correct. So either you are ready to bomb your mind, or it will go the way it always has.

You have to give yourself at least three years and you have to be ready to pay the highest price you have paid so far.

I know I am doing psychological terrorism, but it is not easy, it is very difficult not because of the copy and paste you will make about the marketing ecosystem.

It is hard because of what we are going to talk about right now. You have to realize that if you get no results, you are part of the 99%. You have to be part of the 1%, isolate yourself totally, upset your life. If you are ready to do so, this will bring you success. If you are not ready to do so, everything that comes next will be useless.

We have talked about how to keep the focus, how to reprogram our mind, how to be able to perform actions every day, despite the whole world is against us.

Now let's understand how to take actions and what actions to take.

You have to do is accept that you can fail miserably because you are going to do something totally different from everything you have done so far, you will start driving the car like your first time at the driving school.

This is what will happen: everything you will do will not work and you will live every day thinking about giving up.

At the end of this book you will have the same paradigms you have today. It will start working in a while or maybe it will work immediately, but if your current paradigms row against you, everything you are doing will be destroyed in a way or the other.

I am telling you this because you are currently programmed to achieve the result you have at this precise moment and at the end of this book it will be the same thing.

You have to be aware that all your current actions are correct, but they not congruent with your current paradigms.

So, you have to analyse the data, you have to be objective and you have to look at yourself and at everything you are doing from the outside, i.e. you have to understand that the whole system is fine, but it is watering down somewhere because you have a different paradigm.

Try to identify your paradigm clearly, continue with repetition, reading, podcasts, videos on YouTube and try to get out from your current situation as soon as possible.

Another important thing is asking yourself if you would ever buy something from yourself. That is, would you ever give money to someone like you?

Why should someone come to you?

What can you offer that person today?

How can you help him/her out of the current situation?

What can a person learn from you at 360°?

Your focus should be on improving and refining, analysing data, getting out of yourself, looking at you from the outside, then re-entering, improving and refining again and, most importantly, not calling people to complain.

You don't get paid to take energy from others!

You have to share successes, you have to solve failures by yourself, assuming your own responsibility.

You get and will get what you give; if you give problems you will receive problems, if you give joy and happiness, if you try to help other people, this will be given back to you.

Do not be elegant and kind, people do not buy from polite people, they buy from people who know how to manipulate their brain.

Marketing is nothing more than brain manipulation, as people are not able to make decisions. So, through a whole series of marketing actions, we have to lead them to decide because they are not able to. You do not lead people to make a decision in an elegant way, you rather have to go straight leg on them.

Identify the point of pain they have by digging all the way down; expand the problem and the suffering and then offer the solution, maybe using urgency and scarcity, a whole series of marketing techniques we are going to analyse.

When we have tortured a person to make a decision, we will have to offer them a system that can make them achieve their goals, as I am doing with you right now.

We are actually helping people, but we cannot help them in an elegant way, we help them when we focus on reality.

Also remember that if you let people walk all over you, you will never grow and if you need someone else apart yourself, you will take a big risk, since you are thinking about today's profit and not in the long run.

If you cannot run your own business, you will not be able to succeed, and you will have to teach this to the other people.

If a friend of yours asks you out to have a spritz and you run to him/her, your time will be of little value and your potential customer knows it.

If you are not able to put your phone upside-down without reading it, without looking at it, without touching it for hours, your time will be of little value again.

Your potential client knows this, because all the actions you take will unconsciously lead him to realize that your time has no value; so you will not be able to teach him how to increase his.

Isolation is always the most important part.

If they do not insult you, you are not doing the right thing, and if they are not against you, you are doing something wrong.

Have haters is not cool, but if you are a perfectly useless person, the market does not notice you at all and does not attack you.

If you are a person who correctly identifies the point of pain and pushes hard, I assure you that this will hurt and will not go unnoticed.

Network Marketing Online

You are digging on a wound and when you dig on a wound there are two types of people. Those who will feel the pain and take your solution to solve it, and those who will not want to get out of the situation and will attack you brutally because your success will hurt them, even more than their pain.

People hate you, insult you and attack you because they need you and because you are touching their point of pain.

They insult you because you are doing the right thing. Stopping when you are being insulted is wrong: this is actually something good, since it means that it is working and that you have identified the right niche.

This is the time to go all in.

That is why haters are important.

If a successful person pays you a compliment, that is fine, it is a true compliment, but if someone from the 99% pays you a compliment it cannot be sincere.

Maybe when you were at the same level, you talked to them, you went out together, but now you are slowly moving away, you are destroying relationships. Most people do not see it in a positive way, and that is what you have to feel.

If you do not get this feeling, it is because you are continuing to do things the way you have always done them and you are not going in the right direction.

You have to create an attack plan that is sustainable for three years; it is very important you put yourself in an economically and mentally affordable position.

Unsuccessful people try to invest everything they have in a few months and fail systematically.

If this is your horizon, do not invest at all, close your computer, go to the beach, do not read this book anymore.

You have to create a sustainable attack plan for three years, you have to be able to live well for three years, both economically and mentally.

Network Marketing Online

You have to be able to sustain those small expenses that will be needed to set up your business.

You have to be able to live for three years without earning a single euro, because in this situation you are calm and all you will earn will be a surplus.

You have to reset all unnecessary expenses to invest in assets that can bring you a very high ROI.

Spritz is not an asset, 200€ shoes are not an asset, your car is not an asset, disco nights are not an asset and the list could go on and on.

Most of what you spend money on is not an asset.

If you do not want to invest in the tools necessary for your business, but you go at least once a month to eat a pizza, you are not ready to do business.

People say they do not have any money, but they go out and drink spritz, have aperitifs, buy new shoes, 1000€ phones, etc...

These people are not ready to do business!

If you are objectively incapable of affording expenses right now, ask someone to help you.

It is fair enough that people spend 20% of their budget on uselessness and fun, but if you earn 1000 and you spend 300 or 400 a month on useless things, this is crazy.

You have to understand that if you stop drinking spritz and dedicate that money to develop an asset, tomorrow you will be able to drink 10 spritz and not just 1.

I know you have been told you deserve a vacation every now and then, but you don't.

I have not been on vacation for 8 years, I have worked my ass off investing more than I earned to join training courses and my current results are the result of 8 years of hard work.

Today I often go on vacation because I can afford it, because I worked my ass off and this is the smart way to build a business.

And above all, you must not let yourself be blocked by perfectionism, you will never be ready, everything you do can always be improved, you will improve it day after day, but you have to start.

Every time you fail, you line up your shot, you get better, you change, the important thing is to move on.

The important thing is to learn from that failure and find the solution immediately.

This is the most important thing and you do not have to believe a single word of what I'm saying. Everything I am saying has totally transformed my life and the lives of millions of people around the world, but you have to be the first to be aware of it thanks to daily application.

The only real secret is that the market is ready to pay and the universe is ready to order the market to pay you only in relation to the problems you are able to solve, to the solutions you are able to offer.

Why is a gas station attendant underpaid?

Why is a bricklayer underpaid?

Why are an employee or a secretary underpaid?

Because they can be duplicated and because if the secretary resigns tomorrow, a new secretary will be immediately ready, maybe a prettier one.

On the other hand, if I disappeared tomorrow, all the people around me would be missing something, not because there is no one like me, but because people like me are difficult to duplicate.

We must isolate ourselves, we must change our paradigms and we must not believe everything people say, because we always want to be better than the others. The moment you get involved, the moment you are ready to prove yourself you are better than me, I will be the happiest person in the world.

What you have to do is to take my advice, study, apply and try to improve, try to create something different.

You must be unique and rare, you cannot be the clone of another because you will always get paid like him. We are all limited by the knowledge we have, the paradigms we own. We can all improve; that is why I study and try to overcome myself every day.

Growing up, becoming problem solvers and strengthening our armour will give us the chance to get paid more and more and to achieve maximum success.

CHAPTER 2

IDENTIFY THE CORRECT MARKET NICHE

This is the second section of this book, where we will see exactly how to identify the correct niche market.

Basically, we get paid to do this job, to bring the right product in front of the right niche market through the right marketing action. So all we have to do is to create a system that gives us the possibility to bring our opportunity in front of the right niche market, i.e. in front of people who will use our product or service to achieve their goals that, as I showed you in the previous chapter, are never economic goals.

The main problem for people approaching Network Marketing for the first time is to think that everyone may be interested in what we have to offer. Actually, I could say it is true, but if we do not find the right angle of attack, we will look like sellers who have as their only goal to take home some money without solving our customer's problems.

There are people who want to work with a company in the travel industry because they love travelling and would like to do it at an affordable price. Others would like to find a partner or friends to share the same interests.

They consider this action a vehicle to put people in contact, because there is more chance of finding the right person within an industry where basically people are more advanced, want to grow, study, learn, get something more out of life.

Or this can be a goal for all those people who, like me, have only and exclusively the goal of adding an asset to their business portfolio to diversify and increase their earnings.

It could be an opportunity for a university student who finishes his studies and realizes that he is not ready for the world of work that is coming, the digital one, where automation and social are the master.

So, he realizes that to enter into a totally different sector where there is growth, where there is space and where there are new technologies, he can use our opportunity as a vehicle.

It can also be an opportunity for an entrepreneur, who knows the cost of the employees, of the management of the business, of taxes and of a whole range of problems related to doing business.

The entrepreneur says, "Man, here you give me the chance to start a business at practically no cost, with respect to what can be a real business out there, where we have to buy the building or rent it and furnish it".

Maybe we have a restaurant, a bar and so we have to have the kitchen, the counter, the employees, the accountant. In other words, there is a rather complex management, totally different from the management that can be very simple going to develop this business online.

With these examples you start to understand that, when we develop a business, online or offline, whether it goes to intercept the latent demand of the market, we cannot offer it to everybody: to turn on the light bulb within the brain of our target market we must use levers.

What is the latent question?

There are two types of question, the conscious one and the latent one.

The conscious question is simply the one that comes out of the search engines.

For example, I want to make a Neapolitan coffee because I know that in Naples they do it better, and I want to find out how to make this good Neapolitan coffee.

I google it and type "how to make Neapolitan coffee." This is a conscious question, because at this precise moment I need to know how to make Neapolitan coffee and googling it I will find a whole series of results that represent the supply that goes to intercept my demand.

It is a very strong offer, because at that precise moment I need to know how to make Neapolitan coffee and I have put myself in a position to take advantage of the information that is offered to me.

If I have a cold, a severe sore throat and other symptoms, and then within Google I will type "how to solve this specific cold with certain symptoms". Here, too, you understand that this is a very strong question, because right now I really need to know how to solve my problem.

You don't have to convince me too much, because I need it very much and I just want to understand if you can help me and, if you are, I will buy it directly.

At the same time, there is the latent question, the one that we find on Social.

I may be entering the Social because I am in the bathroom or I am on break at work, maybe I am at the restaurant, I have just ordered my meal and I am waiting for my pasta, so I have a look on Facebook.

In that precise moment, the reason why I find myself inside the Social is to stall, to spend time without having to devote attention to it.

At that time, posts and insertions will appear, a whole series of stuff will pass and capture my attention.

And the only way to catch my attention is to use levers.

Network Marketing Online

This is an opportunity for everyone, but when you work on the latent question, you have to create a connection point, you have to create something that, at that precise moment when I do not need anything, you are able to capture my attention. In this chapter we will see how to capture the attention of our audience.

So, we realize that our market target is no longer our country or the whole world, but is a part of it: it can be the university student, the entrepreneur, the networker, or it can be many small different niches.

I am telling you that you can take anyone, you can have the whole world to recruit, but you'll have to attack it through totally different attack angles.

To make you better understand what 'angle of attack' means, let's have an example with a pair of jeans.

A jeans can be sold to a person who loves Levi's, it can be sold to a person who wants a clear jeans, it can be sold to a person who wants a torn jeans, it can be sold to a person who, at that time, has some sauce on his pants, has to go to a meeting, has no way to go home and change his dresses, so goes to the nearest store to buy a jeans.

I am basically selling the same pants through different angles of attack:

- I satisfy the kid's need to be fashionable through ripped jeans.
- I sell pants to the lover of the brand Levi's.
- I satisfy the urgency of those who have to go to a meeting and need clean pants.
- I satisfy a girl who hates dark jeans and wants them light.

As you can see, I sell the same trousers to totally different people, focusing on specific needs and requirements.

Our job is to identify a specific niche within the largest market and attack it through different angles of attack.

Now let's start to get closer to our business opportunity and let's take another example to better understand the angles of attack.

Network Marketing Online

Let's take a college student to whom we want to offer our project.

He can enter because he has finished his studies and to enter the world of work he realizes that the university course is not able to take him into a totally digitalized world of work.

We can go to an off-site university student who needs to pay the rent, eat a pizza, cover all the expenses, and also to have fun.

His parents give him money for his survival, but he has no money for his free time. So, I am going to pick up the student who wants to live university life at a higher and more comfortable level.

Or I'll sell the project to an economics student, explaining why network marketing will explode in the next few years. When I explain him that 66 million jobs will be lost because of robotics and digitization, that all these people who will be fired will try themselves into the world of catering (because the easiest thing to do according to collective imagination is open a bar or restaurant, or do network marketing), I will certainly catch his interest.

In this way, university students make up my target market, but to take them all and increase my conversion factor, I use the angles of attack to hit different needs.

I am talking to them specifically because I am offering them what they need.

When I do this, I create testimonials of success after the person has become part of my project.

As soon as I enrol a new person, he/she must be immediately placed within an ad hoc training course, capable of leading him/her to the achievement of the objectives that they showed at the beginning.

This is a very important step, because success stories help to recruit new people and show them how similar people have achieved common results.

They are three very simple steps that have a power out of the ordinary:

- Identify the market niche.
- Attach the niche through different angles of attack.
- Create success stories.

When you launch a business, the market analysis is usually much more complex than what I am doing right now, but it is a luxury we can afford in network marketing.

If I launch a brand that aims to sell lawnmowers to gardeners, of course I will have to analyze on search engines if there is a demand that can absorb my product and bring me to be profitable in the long term.

I have to understand how many people there are, how I can reach them, if they are present on Social, in dedicated forums, if I have to send paper letters at home and more.

The market analysis is much more complex, while in our case it is very simple because basically, as we said before, everyone can need you.

Whatever people do in life, they do it to achieve goals, and to achieve these goals they need a means that is always the economic-financial means and we have the means to bring them to be satisfied, so we have the opportunity to work with them.

Just open the window, look outside and realize that any person who passes by is in our niche market.

Obviously, we will work with different angles of attack and we will choose a sub-niche, but we know that it already exists. So we do not have to do all the complex and articulated analysis that is done in case I have to look for people to understand if the product I want to launch makes sense to exist.

Basically, I gave you the main niches, but there are many more that are fine, you just have to find the right angle of attack.

Take for example the niche of those who launch themselves into a new business opportunity and fail miserably.

This niche is made up of people like you who do network marketing.

Network Marketing Online

There may be successful networkers who work in the traditional way, the classic networker who makes the list of names, inviting his friends and family.

There can be a successful networker working online through direct response marketing, identifying the right market strategy, putting the product in front of the right people.

There may be the successful networker who works online organically, using his profile, or goes into groups without doing sponsored campaigns and tries to identify people in a slightly different way.

Then there are the networkers in difficulty, which are the vast majority, about 96%, without a specific strategy.

They started to do network marketing and, unfortunately or fortunately, they started to follow the sponsor who did not give him a well-defined strategy, maybe they simply advised him to make the list of names. So he has already burned all his contacts, and he does not know how to move forward, he has no idea how to generate a contact.

There is the networker who would like to work online, but does not have the faintest idea of how to do it. Maybe he does not have the opportunity to invest in training, because quality training costs thousands of euros.

There are networker opportunity seekers with their asses on the ground, those who have entered into a project simply because someone told him that they could make big money in a short time without doing anything.

And there are the aspiring networkers, who are slowly trying to understand how it all works and why it might make sense to invest time in this business.

Therefore, we have three types of networkers:

- The successful networker.
- The networker in trouble.
- The aspiring networker.

Every one of them needs something different!

Network Marketing Online

The successful networker may want to add a new asset to his business portfolio because if he is successful, and is already earning well, we could be useful to him for flanking an asset.

The networker in difficulty needs a system that allows him to generate contacts and duplicate, the two most important things.

The aspiring networker needs to be completely trained, because he doesn't know anything about this new reality and indoctrination is the process that will lead him to make a decision.

At the moment, you can perfectly understand why everyone fails when they offer business opportunities to networkers: they don't have the faintest idea of who they want to put in the structure, why, what their market strategy is and, most importantly, what to offer them once they have made the most important decision to join.

I have to set up all the communication in relation to which of the three types of networkers I want to recruit.

I will have to educate the successful networker, showing him why he should devote part of his focus to our business opportunity. Then, I will have to show him the industry data, what could be the growth in the coming years and, perhaps, our recruitment system that will lead him to earn without investing too much time, since he needs to reserve his time for his already successful business.

The networker who has difficulty is curious and I understand the reason for his difficulty.

There are people who have a good system in their hands, but cannot close because of shyness.

So I am going to catch them by showing them a system where the final call can be made by someone else.

There will be those who have made the list of names, burned it and no longer have any idea who to call and how to do it. They need to understand the basic laws of marketing, how to identify a market target and structure the right offer to show through the right marketing ecosystem.

Some are in the beauty segment by mistake and fail because they do not believe in the products. Here it will be enough to show a different company, more in line with their propensity and transfer them to the new business opportunity.

In short, everyone is ready to come to us, but we have to show them why and pack the offer in a really attractive way, through an offer that they cannot refuse.

If we know which company they are working with, we can go and disqualify that company as we will see shortly.

If, on the other hand, we have an aspiring networker in front of us, we must make them understand why it is interesting to start this process together, what concrete objectives they can achieve and how our recruitment system works.

It eliminates all that stuff related to the "we are the best", "we are a historical company" and so on.

Just make him understand, objectively, why you, and not the company, have a significantly different offer than your competitors.

If you do not have it and you do not know how to motivate it, you are like all the others and the company you work with will not be able to bring it to the desired results.

There are three main ways to attack a market!

The first by detecting and pressing strongly on the point of pain.

The point of pain is the one that creates the greatest concern to your potential market target.

The networker who is doing network marketing with some companies and with a very fragile team will have a very strong point of pain: the lack of contacts or the lack of time to go and generate contacts constantly day after day. Or the lack of ability to take 50 "no" before reaching a yes, to be treated badly, to be seen as "seller", even if seller is not the right term because for me it is a positive word.

I love people who know how to sell aggressively and manage to manipulate the decision-making processes of the market target.

Network Marketing Online

Sellers are the people who make the most money, so seller is definitely the wrong word.

The seller who wants to sell you without giving you the opportunity to create a real advantage, because he does not have a complex system and still tries to sell you the network marketing as a system to generate a profit, actually feels in trouble knowing that he is the first to fail in this adventure.

We start from a pain and then we slowly move towards the solution, disqualifying the competition.

Disqualifying the competition does not mean talking badly about the companies or products, because the companies are all very good, as are the products.

Maybe there is some company that is a Ponzi scheme, or some product that sucks, but we must never say bad of anyone.

Disqualification means positioning oneself by difference!

For example, I want to disqualify a specific company, I want to work with people who network with a specific company, and pretend that this specific company sells supplements or wellness stuff. I can disqualify it and use the pain to make the networker understand that when he talks to his potential target market, as soon as he understands that he works for a company that sells supplements or beauty products, he will leave without even trying to understand what kind of system it is.

For many years, totally incompetent people have worked in that sector, destroying the market.

So, we are attacking that company without attacking it, shifting the problem to the preconceptions that people have about this type of activity.

In other words, working with this kind of company often encounters very strong barriers.

We are disqualifying the competition and positioning ourselves for difference.

In this case, it becomes much easier, because we do not have to pull out the marketing plan or the product to capture the attention of the networker. We just have to say that he may be the best in the world, but without changing his offer, he will always have to fight against hardly surmountable skepticism.

The third way to attack a market, after locating the point of pain and disqualifying competition, is selling the dream.

I do not like selling the dream, because even if you capture the attention of those who seek the quick and immediate gain, it is still a very important and very strong attack lever that can be used to capture the attention.

However, after recruiting the contact, I always have the opportunity to include it in an educational path that shows him how to achieve the dream working hard, studying, testing and investing in terms of time and money.

Now you are probably wondering with which people to collaborate, whether with entrepreneurs, university students, employees, or networkers.

Let's just say that to answer this question, you need to ask yourself the following:

- What do you do for a living?
- What are your skills?
- Who would you like to help or become?
- Is there any successful person you are inspired by, or who might become your mentor? How does he work? What is he doing?
- In which field you are a number one?
- What is the area of expertise where no one can knock you down?
- Who would you like to work with?

For example, I hate working with people who do not have the slightest entrepreneurial mentality and do not want to invest time and money.

That is why I created all my marketing systems in such a way that I lost these kind of people before I even got to talk to my coaches, or lose them during the education process that leads them to work, if by mistake they managed to pass even the initial funnel.

Network Marketing Online

Let's say that before entering a niche market I analyzed myself trying to figure out who I am and who I want to help.

I want to work with people who have already experienced an important educational path, people who maybe have been to Tony Robbins, who have read "Think And Grow Rich", "The Secret", in short, people willing to pay the price, to isolate themselves and to change.

I want people I can relate to and grow with, as well as transfer my systems to them.

I started to configure the typical person to work with, and a corner of attack has become simply the one that can lead me to disqualify all the competition that works with complicated systems, such as landing pages, chatbots, correspondents and more, to get to a simple 5-step system capable of bringing them to success.

Another angle of attack is aimed at those people who want to create an online business, who have already made training courses, but have not achieved success yet.

Maybe because they have taken part to training courses made by people who had never tested that strategy on their company before selling it and then I'm going to pick up those people who, basically believe in the system and are already trained.

After that, we have to get inside our potential customer to better define him and the main questions are the following:

- Which is your biggest problem?
- What doesn't make you sleep at night?
- What are your five main problems?
- What is stopping you from going from point A to point B?
- You have a goal, but you can't get there. Why?
- Are you single or do you have a family?

This last point is very important, because it affects a whole series of choices and decisions.

- What are the things you believe in right now?

- On the basis of which elements do you make a decision?

- What is your biggest fear?

- What is your financial position?

- How much time do you have?

-

Here we will understand what his problems are, what his desires are, what he lacks to go from point A to point B, whether he is able to make decisions or if he could be influenced by someone, in this case his family.

Maybe he has kids, two or three kids, so it is hard for him to start a new business.

If you have time or if you are working from morning to night, if you are working as an employee all week.

A whole series of topics that will lead us to better define the angle of attack.

We must have someone in front of us, we must see it, because if we do not see it and if we do not know who we are talking to, we do not know what levers to use and we do not know how to structure everything.

We do not know how to make the most of this journey.

You have to understand if he has money and if he is willing to invest it, if he can invest it or if someone complains, if he has to do it secretly, if what we offer can destroy a relationship, and if we really are able to improve his situation.

Another very important point is to throwaway all the things he believes in to structure the best path to help him.

For example, this person has to pay a thirty-year mortgage and has realized (because of the crisis) that he cannot change his job. He knows that his income is now destined to the extinction of this debt. It is absolutely necessary to educate him and to make him understand that what he believes is wrong, supporting him with concrete facts, and secondly to be able to offer a service capable of helping him to improve this situation.

Having a clear image gives you the chance to dramatically increase your closing rate.

Imagine having in front of you a girl who tries to be an Influencer on Instagram, what are her characteristics?

Usually she is a person who likes to mask his insecurities, to mask the fact that inwardly she knows nothing or almost nothing.

By creating a strong online positioning, she tries to balance all the gaps it has in her real life.

This is usually the average Influencer.

A person who influences social issues but does not influence real life.

So all these girls, who have 40/50 thousand followers on Instagram, have a strong problem, that is insecurity.

They are not even shamelessly oriented to selling because they are afraid, they do not know how to sell and they always try to take a small percentage of clothes or products that they promote by pretending to advise.

These people will be attracted only and exclusively by making them believe that your product will serve to turn them even more into stars and have greater visibility, further feeding their ego.

It is useless for you to try and explain them that it is better to create a solid business than to sell products for 20€, because it is not in their sphere of interest and you will be resoundingly rejected.

Now imagine you have in front of you an engineer or an architect, with rectangular glasses, a very analytical person. Such a person, dressed up with his shirt buttoned almost to the top, very schematic and lover of order and mathematics, will want to know what is the ROI, and we must give him company data, we must show him why investing in our company makes sense.

- What is the potential market target?
- What could be the future growth?
- What are the company's balance sheets?
- What do the rating agencies say?

- Is the marketing plan sustainable?

Imagine a businessman with a cup of coffee in front of him, maybe one who invests in parallel assets, who has many successful assets and earns from many sources and has many managers working for him.

He does round tables to find out if it makes sense to invest in a new business or not.

In this case, everything we have said before does not make any sense, because you can catch someone like this by saying that he can invest €10,000 in sponsored campaigns over a certain period of time, using a tested system, and have a certain type of ROI.

This person wants to know how much he has to pull out and how much he comes back, he does not want to get his hands on it and study, he simply invests.

Finally, imagine a girl who maybe goes out with people who have a BMX, a skateboard, who do freestyle and have fun. She is a bit against the schemes, against over-regulation, against the law, against the government and against the whole system.

She wants to be free, different from the others, and against everything and everyone.

In this case, she will buy a system that will give her the opportunity to meet other people, live in total freedom, carry out her ideals, using a vehicle that can lead many other people to live free, outside the regulation and oppression of traditional jobs and becoming a promoter of this philosophy.

Now do you understand why everyone fails when they promote a business opportunity?

They offer what they want to offer without considering whether the person in front of them is willing to buy.

If you want to take giant steps in this business, the most important thing to do is to structure a type of communication that differs each time depending on the person you are facing and the needs he/she has.

CHAPTER 3

PACKAGE OFFER

Once you're clear on how to work on the mindset to become an extremely successful person and you understand the importance of correctly identifying the right market niche, we can move on to creating the offer.

This is another step where everyone falls, thinking that the business opportunity may be enough to bring your customers to get results.

If you understand that everyone needs to reach a non-economic goal through an economic means, you know at the same time that you have to offer a system capable of taking it from point A to point B.

For example, if you work with a company that sells water, and you're recruiting a person who has to pay off a mortgage, putting a bottle of water in her hand will not change her situation, because you're selling a dream that is not based on solid foundations.

You need to create a sustainable marketing ecosystem that can lead anyone to achieve goals through the sale of the bottle of water.

The reason he's choosing you and not another one is for the system and not for the company you're working with.

Networkers are afraid that someone else will take away their contact, because they know very well that after recruiting a representative, the latter will go out after a few months as attracted by an ephemeral dream.

If you get into one of my funnels, you know exactly what I mean when I talk about system.

You can access it by clicking on the following link:

https://bit.ly/dwtexpansion

When people leave me their contact, I show them my marketing ecosystem through a video.

I explain the 5 essential points around which the whole construction of the business revolves:

1. Reference market.

2. Product offered.

3. Customer acquisition system.

4. Advanced backend training.

5. Customer service.

Point 2 relates to the business opportunity, i.e. the product of the company I work with; all the rest is the real advantage I have with respect to my competitors, because I offer the chance to win.

In this presentation, I explain that to be successful in this business you need to correctly identify a thirsty crowd, ready to buy from us.

I explain why I chose to collaborate with this specific company, rather than another, and I show numbers to support my thesis.

I show everything that is my customer acquisition system, which brings me every day a constant flow of contacts interested in what I offer, and everything that happens after a potential customer decides to become a customer and collaborate with me.

The fourth point is reassuring, as I show my training program to be sold to people who decide to start a career in the network marketing segment, a program that those who work with me will get for free.

Finally, the customer service will eliminate all the problems related to the management of downlines, because you can always count on a team formed to manage anyone.

Now you understand the huge difference between choosing to work with me rather than someone else and what you'll have to do if you really want to be successful is simply replicate this system.

Offer the people you recruit, and who will recruit the boys in your team, a training program that will lead them to achieve results in the shortest possible time and support capable of forming the downlines, even if they will not be able to do it themselves.

You can't leave anything to chance and you can't afford to leave the power to others because, if one day someone decides to leave, you will lose part, if not all, of their team.

If you are always leading and being seen as the undisputed leader, you will always have the strength to tie people to your figure, bypassing any other leader in your downline.

I know this has its pros and cons, but the time will come when they will join your networker team with the sole aim of making quick profits and then looting as much as possible.

You can only avoid this by working on your authority, always strengthening your brand and your leadership.

I also know that, most likely, right now you're wondering how you can make a system like that from scratch.

First of all, this book will be of great help to you, as it will give you the opportunity to structure your business in a solid and profitable way. After that, you can go in depth using the available training courses.

However, the basic concept is to start generating the first results.

Implement the marketing ecosystem as you are learning right now and enroll the first people who will help you increase revenue and see if your system is solid or if it's watering somewhere.

The next step is to collect their success stories to speed up the recruitment process, teach them how to work, perhaps advising them to buy this book, and start recording your video lessons that explain to new distributors how to work from the moment of registration.

This is the most important step, which will give you an important advantage over all your competitors who just use corporate training material.

You need to be perceived as a top expert in the field and, above all, as a trainer or consultant, because most of the people you recruit won't know how to do and will come from a completely failed experience, so you will be their light.

They are choosing you for this reason and you can't risk disappointing them or not turning them into success stories.

The starting moment is crucial for you, because it will help you to create your own positioning and the story that will be told by your downline.

When they try to recruit and work on a daily basis, they can count on you to tell the story of a person who has created something immense and who has allowed a certain number of people to achieve success.

This kind of story is very powerful to sell the business opportunity, and it is much more important than telling the story of the company you work with because, most of the time, nobody really cares about it.

They want to know that you started from zero and that you made it, that you were like them and that you have overcome important obstacles to build an offer capable of avoiding the same obstacles now that they have decided to embark on this new adventure.

Don't cradle yourself and don't take advantage of the shadow of your upline or your sponsor, don't live in his shelter, but get involved and create your own reality because as long as you are under his protection you will never get better results.

You have to create your own success story to be told, and you have to create a complex system in which you insert the company you work with. Otherwise your offer will be too weak and unattractive, and you'll take the risk to get lost in the chaos of the networkers trying in vain to get to the end of the month.

Above all, make it as easy as possible and remember to enclose your offer within a single and unique link.

You must pack the offer in such a way that, when your downline goes to sell it, it will deliver a link through which the new agents can start this path.

For example, I have a link to a form created in my autoresponder, where people enter their full name, email address and phone number to receive daily, for seven days, video lessons that will allow them to replicate my own marketing ecosystem.

At the end of the 7 days, they will receive access to the private Facebook group where they will find the members of the customer service and all the other people who are working using the same system. Moreover, they will be able to create their own private access to a member area where I constantly upload new video lessons.

This simplicity makes the system duplicable, as people know that they only have to work on the generation of contacts and not on everything that happens afterwards.

If you can erase the problem of having to train each person, and you can save their time, your structure will be able to grow quickly and solidly.

In addition, the system you provide must be offered for sale to all people who do not or will not do business with you, because during the negotiation they must know that they are receiving some training value for free, only because they will make the decision to cooperate with your team.

Give your guys an important value they can play with to make it easier for them to close sensitive contacts.

If an uninfluential guy is talking to a successful person, he can leverage the system and the team to talk on an equal footing and maybe register a proxy who in other ways would have been burned in less than five minutes.

Each person in your downline has a degree of influence ranging from 0 to 10 and the more people with a high degree of influence, the deeper your structure can go.

The real problem is that most people have a degree of influence below the average value and, for this reason, it will be almost impossible to recruit strong networkers or influential people in any other sector.

This is normal, because everyone aspires to work with strong people from whom we can grow, improve and learn every day.

Network Marketing Online

That's why you have to turn your weakest networkers into messengers who will carry your word around and who will simply be the bridge capable of carrying diamonds to you.

This strategy will help you achieve two goals at once:

1. Giving the weakest a chance to compete with the strongest.
2. Increase your authority, as everyone else will see your people in charge as coaches working for your brand.

Everybody would like to get an autograph of our favourite star and everybody like to deal with successful people. So treat yourself as you were a successful person and put yourself in the spotlight, your business will greatly benefit from it.

CHAPTER 4

ANATOMY OF A MARKETING ECOSYSTEM

Once you have structured your offer correctly, we can proceed to the creation of our marketing ecosystem, but first you need to understand what is the goal to be achieved.

In our case, a marketing ecosystem must:

- Identify a potential customer.
- Call his attention.
- Prequalify or de-qualify.
- Insert the customer into the training system and start over.

The first step is reached by using Social, through the use of an organic or sponsored system, i.e. the creation of advertising campaigns to bring target audience to our pages.

To draw their attention, instead, you must use the analysis of your niche market, press on the point of pain, disqualify your competitors or use a great promise that leads them to perceive that they can achieve their goals.

After that, we enter the heart of the system that will have to prequalify and disqualify and if at this moment you are a little confused, don't worry because I will explain immediately what it means.

Pre-qualify means creating a series of contents that have the ability to make your potential customer in target with your offer, or to make him understand what you do and how you work, so as to bring him to talk to you only for the final details.

Disqualifying, even more important than prequalifying, is instead the action that removes or prevents all the people you want to have nothing to do with from passing through.

If you want to be successful in network marketing and build a solid team, especially avoid talking every day with useless people who will only waste your time, you have to build a system to prevent these people from passing.

Surely you've been told to make short presentation videos, four or five minutes, because people have a low threshold of attention and because they get bored easily.

I know because I have been told too, bullshit!

If you try to be for everyone and bring everybody to the end of your funnel, you're wasting time and you're telling the market that your value equals zero.

The videos must last at least half an hour, and we'll see soon and everything you write or say must discourage more than encourage, must hold back and carry on only the warriors.

Have you ever read anywhere in this book so far that you click on any buttons and you get money?

Have you read somewhere that it's easy and painless?

Have you ever read that network marketing is an activity for everyone, that makes you earn in a few months and that you can carry on with a few hours a week?

Or you've been bombed by the importance of the mindset and the probability of failure, which is terribly higher than the probability of success?

Here's what you have to do, psychological terrorism, because you want to devote your precious time to people who are willing to create a great legacy and not to the opportunity seeker on duty.

You will never be able to work with professionals if you have a system for amateurs, and you will never be able to duplicate if you do not have professionals in structure.

Having said that, I can start showing you my marketing ecosystem capable of holding back everything you don't need and getting the best out of it, so let's get on with it.

It is a system that consists of 6 steps:

1. Lead generation.
2. Opt-in page.
3. Video sales letter.
4. Survey.

5. Strategic consulting.

6. Backend training.

We are talking about a Video Sales Letter funnel, that is a system that converts through indoctrination that takes place through video.

So, in the first phase we generate traffic to bring inside the optin page, and we can generate this traffic, as already mentioned, in an organic or paid way and I'll show you later how to do it.

Then we bring the people within the first page that will serve, further after the first approach by advertisement or by the organic method, to show what they will receive and if they are targeted with our offer.

If so, they will leave their details, which are usually full name and email address, and they will go to the second page containing the video, which I will show you here how to do it best.

After looking at it, they will pass through a third page where they will have to answer a series of questions that will allow us to understand who we are dealing with.

The questions I use are:

Q: What kind of person are you?

A: I complain all the time and pretend to earn money without going to work.
A: I love to learn and grow continuously in every aspect of my life.

Q: Why do you want to start this business?

A: Because I love building something great.
A: I'm only interested in money, cars and good life.

Q: What kind of entrepreneur do you prefer?

A: One who tries to earn by exploiting other people.
A: One who struggles every day to achieve his goals and invests, creating more and more value.

Q: What's your current situation?

A: Student.

A: Employee.

A: Entrepreneur.

A: Freelancer.

A: Unemployed.

A: Other.

Q: What is your net monthly turnover target?

A: Up to 1000€.

A: From 1000€ to 3000€.

A: From 3000€ to 5000€.

A: Over 5000€.

Q: When you are facing a challenge, how do you behave?

A: I panic.

A: I remain calm, I analyze all potential solutions and attack.

Q: If you could achieve your goal after learning something new, what would you do?

A: I would give up because I don't want to learn anymore, I'm fed up.

A: I would learn and apply everything, I need to grow and earn.

Network Marketing Online

Q: Do you have resources to invest in your business?

A: Absolutely not.
A: I can afford to invest a little bit if I get back fast enough.
A: I can invest everything I need.

Q: What statement do you feel closest to you?

A: I want to work a little but until I retire.
A: I'm willing to work hard for a few years to live the rest of my life in freedom.

At the end they can ask for a 30-minute strategic consultancy with one of my coaches and if they don't show up without having warned them of the problem that won't lead them to make the call, they simply can't do it anymore if they don't pay 665€.

This is because time is the most precious resource, much more important than money, and if someone is not able to respect it, he can go and work with someone else, because I do not want to have anything to do with this kind of people.

As you can see, the system is articulated, long and it discourages people precisely because it disqualifies and only brings the cream to the end.

The penultimate step is related to strategic consulting; there will be a script to follow to bring the contact to take the decision to love it or least it, avoiding receiving answers such as "maybe" or "I must think about it". After that, the training path will begin, if the contact will have decided to work with us.

One very important thing is also to remove as many objections as possible, so as to make the work of your downline in strategic consulting much easier.

To remove objections you have only one way, move the focus.

Objections arise on the presentation you have made. For this reason by including the business opportunity in a more complete offer and discounting to zero the training program to those who will enter after the call in your team, you will bring the potential customer to ask only how it will be structured and details about everyday life.

It is much easier to remove objections than to teach your team how to handle them, as each objection hides behind another much larger one and becomes a game of chess that will lead to the real objection and the closure of the negotiation.

So, before we talk about how to generate traffic to bring to our pages, let's see how to structure a presentation video that is capable of converting.

The duration of the video must be between 45 and 60 minutes.

You can even shorten it to 30 minutes, but it is risky, because the goal is to provide everything your contact needs to make a decision.

There will be three parts in the video:

The first one will serve to create connection and excite.

It is the part that makes up 26% of the video and serves to fully capture the attention by selling the video itself, i.e. making it clear to your potential customer that you are the right person to talk to him and this is the offer that he was looking for a long time.

The second part, which takes 53% of the video, is used to show those who are listening to you that through your offer can bridge the gap between point A and point B.

Remember that the content does not show how cool the company or your offer is, but rather how much everything you are presenting is able to lead it to solve a problem.

The last part, which takes 21%, serves to sell the strategic advice, bring him to act immediately to talk with one of the coaches so that he can understand how to make this offer unique so that it can achieve its goal in a given time.

I know that your temptation will be to eliminate the advice and put the sale of the opportunity directly, but I strongly advise against it, because it will reduce the conversion rate and increase the incubation period of the lead.

Network Marketing Online

Few people are able to make a decision instantly, most need to think about it and the best thing is to make them think before the advice, so as to conclude the negotiation on the phone in one fell swoop, without wasting time.

If you have well structured the video (and I recommend you to watch mine using the link -> https://bit.ly/dwtexpansion), your contacts will not come in consultation to get more information, and he will immediately buy, because he already got the information.

Long videos always win against short videos, so never believe people who tell you to shorten or that the attention threshold is low.

The attention threshold is low for those who have no interest, for all the others even a 3-hour video would be fine.

There are television series that last years and no one has ever complained about this, we live every day waiting to watch the next episode and devour all the content.

Your only focus should be on the few interested people who will listen to what you have to say with a lot of attention, and who will also take notes because these are the only people who will fill your pockets, all the others will only serve to create greater engagement with your business.

Mark these things I'm telling you and never fall into the trap of wanting to be for everyone because, I'm sure, your sponsor and your upline will always and only push you to talk to anyone.

CHAPTER 5

SOURCES OF TRAFFIC

Now let's talk about organic traffic, starting with its definition.

Organic traffic is what you send within your contact capture page without using paid traffic sources. It can be generated online and/or offline.

The best way to generate organic offline traffic is by doing what you've always done, but by bringing all your contacts to talk to you about their point of pain.

One of the things human beings love most is to talk about problems, difficulties, fears and obstacles, so we make this drama profitable.

Go and have a coffee with them, meet them all one by one, go out and interact, let them talk about everything that goes wrong and, as soon as you have the chance, show the solution.

Take them inside your funnel, where you'll have them enter the data and keep talking about other things, so you don't seem interested in showing your project.

You will have all the emails you send to your mailing list to follow up, the retargeting on Facebook, the one on WhatsApp, the paper you send home and all the possible and imaginable material.

Once captured the contact will be bombed continuously until the day he decides to register.

That's all you have to do, without inventing anything or using trick strategies.

As far as online traffic is concerned we will obviously use Facebook, but before showing you the strategy, let me make sure that your profile is capable of attracting traffic.

First of all you need to have a profile photo where you are there, better with no glasses, so you can look in the eyes who is about to enter.

You need a well edited cover photo that gives a sense of freedom, that makes people imagine life to be lived once they reach their goal.

Logically, it would not be useful to say it, but I've seen things that we humans can't even imagine, your profile will be called with your name and surname, without bullshit and various symbols.

In the description, include something that captures the attention and everything you've done in life that can be positive and appropriate to what you're about to promote.

Then, you have to:

- Remove from your Facebook profile all that is negative (wars, murders, politics and all kinds of black news).
- Delete all posts related to gossip.
- Eliminate kittens, dogs, children (if not yours), country parties and everything that 99% of people publish.

- If after this cleaning operation, your profile will remain empty, publish at least 7 posts with valuable content that your niche would like to read (use your own photos or take them on pixabay.com, never use images taken from Google or images not in high definition).

At this point we are ready to start looking for people, so we will proceed by asking for access to all groups where your potential customers will be present.

Once you are logged in, select at least 30 people a day to add as friends and, only after they have accepted you, send the message to start the conversation by going straight to the point.

An example of a message to be sent is as follows:

Hi... nice to meet you.

My name..., I asked for your friendship because... and I peered at your profile a little.

Network Marketing Online

I have developed a service that helps ... to ... and in the testing phase we have obtained excellent results.

Would you like to use it?

Here you simply explain the real reason why you asked for friendship and start the conversation.

I'm talking about a real reason because, logically, to choose the 30 profiles per day to ask for friendship, you'll go inside their message boards and select the best ones that will strike you for some reason.

All the people who say "no" to you must bring you at least 3 contacts, so always ask to give you these contacts of people they think might be interested, the first that come to mind.

Ask for friendship now and start the conversation in the same way, indicating that it was ... to give you his name and, even here, any other "no" must bring you at least 3 contacts.

As for Instagram it works more or less the same way, with the only difference that you will have to enter a nice description in Bio with a call to action strong to bring contacts to click on the link under the Bio.

This link will obviously lead to your opt-in page.

Before you start working, follow the same instructions I gave you for Facebook to clean your profile and then start looking for contacts.

- Look inside for them in hashtags that your niche would use.
- Post photos using about fifteen hashtags of your niche and vary them with each photo.
- Do not send automatic messages, but check manually each new person who follows you.
- Select at least 30 people per day to follow.
- Only if they also begin to follow you parts with the message to start the conversation, going straight to the point.

Many people use, besides Facebook and Instagram, other social networks including LinkedIn, but I'm not telling you about it because I don't use them and I don't want to talk to you about something I've never done before.

My advice is to always test and vary your messages and your attitude according to the answers you will receive because, of course, we are all different and each of us is more or less good using one strategy rather than another.

The same goes for the sources of paid traffic, which are nothing more than advertising campaigns made with the aim of bringing traffic within our pages, promoting posts that are able to capture the attention of people.

In this case, everything we said when we talked about the angles of attack is very useful to you.

I show you some posts below that I created to promote my project:

This is to leverage the pain of people who have been burned by those who made them believe that it is possible to live on automatic annuities without doing anything.

It's great to think you can live a life on the beach with a few cocktails in your hand while watching your bank account go up...

...but unfortunately it's going to go down terribly steep!

If you get dozens of posts on your wall every day that promise this lifestyle, it's because the world is full of opportunity-seekers who want to earn fast and do nothing.

The problem is that these people do not stand the long term because:

- *They don't feel like working*
- *They don't have the slightest willingness to study*
- *They do not have adequate financial resources*

For this reason, focusing a business on this target will perhaps lead to instantaneous gains but never to constant and predictable growth.

In other words, you will never climb your business and you will never be really free!

So we decided to create a FREE VIDEO LESSON where we show exactly the 5 steps necessary to create your business and make it immediately duplicable and scalable.

Click on "find out more" and download this video lesson for free.

TITLE: Automatic annuities do not exist!

Or this that leverages the dream, the great promise we make to them:

Finally unveiled the secret system of the DreamWorkers Team...

... "5 steps to create an online business from scratch using freedom and fun as a vehicle to grow"

We are a group of young people who in the last year has helped over 700 people to have more time and the opportunity to live in every part of the world.

We have developed a simple and scalable system, capable of leading anyone to achieve their goals and live the desired life.

So we decided to create a FREE VIDEO LESSON where we show you exactly all the steps needed to create your business that works even while you sleep.

Click on "find out more" and download this video lesson for free.

TITLE: Create your online activity through freedom and fun

This one still goes, instead, to disqualify my competition:

Did they tell you that to make an online business you need chatbots, very complicated funnels and endless email sequences?

Don't worry, that's all they taught us at the beginning of our career in information marketing, but nothing is more wrong.

The only way to be successful and earn consistently and predictably is to have a simple system focused on a single point.

So we decided to make a FREE VIDEO LESSON where we show exactly the 5 steps needed to create your business that works even while you sleep.

Click on "find out more" and download this video lesson for free.

TITLE: Earn more by working less

Then I'll show you two very powerful ones that I used for a different funnel that, most likely, will be the content of another book that will explain what are the issues of advertising campaigns and how to be sure of success.

Here I am leveraging the strong pain of the Networkers:

"I have to think about it"

"I have to ask my partner"

"I don't have any money."

These are the main objections that accompany you every day from morning until evening.

Endless exhausting and stressful days in which you are totally absorbed by this vortex of negative energy that comes out of every phone call, Skype or Zoom.

And the thing that hurts the most is that all this happens not because the person you're talking to "doesn't understand anything", "is obtuse", "doesn't see that the future is in the Network and in the Affiliations" and so on...

...but because you're selling a product to a person you told to offer a system and who needs a system.

I repeat!

You're selling a product to a person you told to offer a system and who needs a system.

I'll make it easy for you:

The person you're talking to and trying to close (assuming they're most likely not on target because they've been generated with names or spam lists) has a GAP between their desired and current situation, which means they need a certain amount of money every month to live better.

And logically, a person who has a problem buys a solution, but...

(... and this is the key...) you are not offering it!

You are selling the opportunity to be free through the company you are working with, which means that you are giving a bottle of water to a person saying to sell it without teaching them how to sell it, without the company doing so and, even worse, saying that there is not to sell but only to share.

If you've read so far... now tell me... what are we talking about?

Did you realize that the objections are normal and that even a rhinoceros in heat would make her?

Do you understand that there is less than nothing congruent about this process?

Did you realize that jumping on chairs and tearing off your hair isn't lead generation?

Did you understand that to earn money you have to sell and not share and, above all, you have to underline it as well as say it immediately?

Do you understand that I could go on for hours and hours and hours?

Good.

Dreamworkers Team

In this case you can click below and finally understand how to create a system capable of charging you for the presentations you make, avoiding making the biggest mistake that all the fake gurus out there are hiding from you.

=> http://bit.ly/dreamworkersreclutator

TITLE: Do you want to close 50% of the calls? Start selling a system and get paid!

Here I disqualify fake gurus:

Did the fake Network Marketing gurus tell you to stop with the Names List and start working with Online Recruitment Funnels?

Too bad that they are hiding from you the real problem behind this methodology, which is revealed as the Names List, totally unsuccessful for you and highly lucrative for them.

I am Matteo Di Febbo, Founder of the DREAMWORKERS TEAM, and in the first 9 months of activity I have enrolled more than 700 people in charge, using this system, more than

85% of whom are totally unable to duplicate and, even if they make you pass this thing as normal, it is not at all.

To have to annihilate hundreds of people at a time to get to the next "diamond", which will annihilate even more than you, thus earning on a sea of people who will not catch a single penny in their entire career, in my opinion, is not the best strategy.

Especially if you consider the huge waste of time you have every day in presenting and trying to convince people totally off target!

For this reason I have created a system that allows you to overcome this obstacle that everyone is hiding from you and that allows you to be paid for the presentations you make.

Click below to receive the free 40-minute video lesson I have prepared for you!

=> http://bit.ly/dreamworkersreclutator

TITLE: Have you been told to leave Name List and switch to Online Funnels?

Surely these advertisements will be useful for you to understand how to best structure the text and able to capture the attention and suck the contact within the path that will bring it up to strategic advice.

Below I also attach three ads that I created to generate traffic within the university niche, so as to bring them into the same system that I showed you, but with a different video created specifically for them.

In this first advertisement I rely on the generic testimony of other students:

Do you know that many university students have started their own online business to have more revenue during their studies and find a business ready for the future?

We all know it... you have so many tests to do and bumps in your head that you don't have a moment of time for yourself and to ask yourself if everything you're doing is correct.

Actually, it is. You can rest easy.

The University offers a complete course of study that serves to acquire all the basic knowledge.

Network Marketing Online

The only problem is that, often, there is a lack of specialist knowledge that, today, is important to bring home real numbers.

How many smart kids do you know who find themselves years old doing free or underpaid internships or, worse still, making photocopies without learning anything?

Over the next few years more than 66 million jobs will be burned due to robotics and digitization and most of the jobs for which we are studying today will no longer exist.

For this reason, starting a parallel online business, which gives you the ability to create an asset that can make you earn in a time-independent manner and gives you the opportunity to have a job that can last forever, is extremely important.

So we decided to make a FREE VIDEO LESSON where we show exactly the 5 steps needed to create your business that works even while you sleep.

Click on "find out more" and download this video lesson for free.

TITLE: University students like you have started this new online activity!

LINK DESCRIPTION: You know that many university students have joined the DREAMWORKERS TEAM and have...

In this second one, I'm playing on the big promise:

Finally unveiled the system that is allowing University Students throughout Italy to build an online business and generate income without affecting the time needed for exams.

According to the study "Automation, skills use and training" signed by the OECD, robots and artificial intelligence will put at risk more than 66 million jobs in the member countries of the organization.

Most of the young people are studying to find work in a world of work that will no longer exist.

For this reason, starting a parallel online business, which gives you the ability to create an asset that can make you earn in a time-independent manner and gives you the opportunity to have a job that can last forever, is extremely important.

So we decided to make a FREE VIDEO LESSON where we show exactly the 5 steps needed to create your business that works even while you sleep.

Click on "find out more" and download this video lesson for free.

You'll find out how some of them managed to score over 30K in the first 516 days.

TITLE: The secret that successful University Students will never want to share!

LINK DESCRIPTION: You know that many university students have joined the DREAMWORKERS TEAM and have...

And in the latter, he relies on pain:

Finding yourself after 5 years or more of university to make free photocopies is not the best!

And if you think it might be a sad reality, know that in the future it will be even worse...

... according to the study "Automation, skills use and training" signed by the OECD, robots and artificial intelligence will put at risk more than 66 million jobs in member countries of the organization.

Most of the young people are studying to find work in a world of work that will no longer exist.

For this reason, starting a parallel online business, which gives you the ability to create an asset that can make you earn in a time-independent manner and gives you the opportunity to have a job that can last forever, is extremely important.

So we decided to make a FREE VIDEO LESSON where we show exactly the 5 steps needed to create your business that works even while you sleep.

Click on "find out more" and download this video lesson for free.

You'll find out how some of them managed to score over 30K in the first 516 days.

TITLE: You are not studying to make photocopies!

LINK DESCRIPTION: You know that many university students have joined the DREAMWORKERS TEAM and have...

Once you have in mind the scheme, the niche and the various attack points, you can create as many combinations as you want and hit each person in the best possible way.

The goal is to arouse interest and bring the contact to consume the content until the strategic advice, in which you will use the following script that will help you to close as many negotiations as possible.

So, without wasting time, let's start to see how to deal with these contacts that have just requested the call.

First of all, I suggest you send them a message as soon as you have received the completed questionnaire.

Something like that's fine:

Dreamworkers Team

Hi...! I am ..., Coach of the DREAMWORKERS TEAM.

I am sending you this message because I have received your 30-minute free Strategic Consultancy application questionnaire worth €665.

The next availabilities are:

- *Today: 17:00/17:30/19:00/20:00*
- *Tomorrow: 13:00/14:30/17:00/19:30*
- *The day after tomorrow: 12:00/13:30/14:00/18:30*

Can you tell me one of these or do you need to select a different time?

And continue with a message like that as soon as you receive a reply:

Andrea then confirm you the Strategic Consultancy for Tuesday, September 8 at 19:30.

Take 30 minutes and make sure you're in a quiet place.

I'm sure you've already watched the free video lesson that he sent you ..., otherwise make sure to watch it before the Call, otherwise it will not be useful and I can only do it once.

Here's the link:

=> ....

Tuesday

This second message is very important because there are some people who reserve the call, but who actually have only watched a piece of video and this must not happen at all because the call serves to close.

I speak to you from experience in the field and with data in hand because I saw the huge difference between a strategic call made as I teach you, after the contact has looked carefully at the presentation video, and a simple presentation call.

Having 5 minutes to try to close a contact after presenting, in which we are both tired, and having 30 full minutes in a call reserved only for closing are not at all the same thing.

CHAPTER 6

SCRIPTS TO USE FOR THE CALL

The script that we will use in strategic consulting will serve to bring the contact towards the immediate closure of the negotiation.

Here's the script:

[BREAK THE INITIAL ICE AND BRING OUT ALL THE SUNSHINE]

Hi ..., I'm ..., how are you? You all right?

Where do you live?

[WAIT FOR HIM TO ANSWER AND CONNECT USING THAT SPECIFIC PLACE, TELLING YOU THE LAST TIME YOU WERE THERE OR ASKING ABOUT WHAT TO VISIT STATING THAT THAT PLACE HAS LONG BEEN ON YOUR LIST]

Okay, we want to start this strategic consultancy, what do you say?

[YOU'RE WAITING FOR ME TO ANSWER]

Perfect! The aim is to understand, through a series of questions, whether our product can be right for you.

If I understand that he can't help you, I'll tell you right away and explain why, otherwise it's up to you at the end of the call to decide whether to take this path with us.

Okay?

[WAIT FOR HIM TO ANSWER AGAIN, ACQUIRE THE YESES AND THE OKES SERVES TO PREPARE YOUR CONTACT TOWARDS THIS KIND OF ANSWER AND MOVE IT FURTHER AND FURTHER AWAY FROM A POTENTIAL NO]

[GO STRAIGHT TO THE POINT OF PAIN WITHOUT WASTING TIME - IF HE ASKED FOR STRATEGIC ADVICE AND ALSO ANSWERED THE CALL IS BECAUSE THERE IS SOMETHING IN HIS LIFE THAT HURTS - IF HE ASKED FOR STRATEGIC ADVICE OUT OF CURIOSITY IS BECAUSE WHAT HE IS DOING RIGHT NOW IS NOT THE BEST, OTHERWISE HE

WOULD HAVE AVOIDED WASTING TIME - WHATEVER THE REASON, HE HAS A PROBLEM AND YOU NEED TO KNOW IT]

In the meantime, I want to share with you immediately a fact that shows you the enormous potential that you have inside. I do Strategic Consultancy every day and, on average, only 8% of those who have left the data arrive to fill in the questionnaire and request the Call.

They are always the most decisive people and it's no wonder they get results! What made you come here?

[OFTEN WHAT SHE ANSWERS IS NOT THE REAL REASON, IF SHE'S NOT ALREADY IN TUNE WITH YOU, SO ASK QUESTIONS AND DIG DEEP UNTIL YOU GET TO THE BIGGEST PAIN - THEN FIND A WAY TO BUILD A BRIDGE THAT ENDS IN HER WORK OR HER CURRENT SITUATION]

What is your job...?

CONTINUE WITH THE QUESTIONS AND KEEP IT ON THE PAIN - YOU SHOULDN'T HAVE ANY

DIFFICULTY BECAUSE PEOPLE LIKE TO COMPLAIN AND TELL ABOUT ALL KINDS OF PROBLEMS - AND WHEN IT'S OPEN ENOUGH...]

How much do you make on average every month?

[DON'T SKIP THIS QUESTION FOR ANY REASON IN THE WORLD BECAUSE IT'S IMPORTANT TO UNDERSTAND HOW MUCH IT WILL TAKE YOUR SYSTEM TO TAKE IT TO THE NEW STEP IT WANTS TO TAKE]

Based on *what you're telling me, how much more do you need to make each month?*

[WAIT FOR HIM TO ANSWER AND THEN DO THE MATH WITH HIM ASKING FOR CONFIRMATION - ALWAYS COLLECT AFFIRMATIVE ANSWERS, WHENEVER YOU CAN]

So you're earning TOT and you still need TOT, which means earning TOT per month. Correct?

[YOU'RE WAITING FOR ME TO ANSWER]

[AT THIS MOMENT YOU HAVE TO FIND OUT IF HE HAS ALREADY DONE OR IS DOING SOMETHING TO FILL THIS GAP OR YOU ARE THE ONLY PERSON HE HAS ADDRESSED FOR THE FIRST TIME - THIS MAKES YOU UNDERSTAND IF HE HAS ALREADY DONE SOMETHING SIMILAR AND HAS NOT SUCCEEDED FOR SOME REASON]

Have you already done something to try to earn these additional TOTs each month? What is it that has kept you from achieving this goal?

[ANSWER ASPECTS]

How important is this goal to you? How would that change things?

[YOUR GOAL IS TO MAKE HIM GO BACK AND FORTH, BRING HIM FROM PAIN TO IMAGINE THE DESIRED SITUATION IN THE FUTURE AND WHEN HE'S IMAGINING IT BRING HIM BACK TO PAIN AGAIN TO MAKE HIM FEEL HOW MUCH IT HURTS]

Okay..., I would say that if you are really determined and you want to grow we can work safely on this goal.

Can I explain how our program works?

[YOU'RE WAITING FOR ME TO ANSWER]

Perfect...! As you have already seen in a summary way in the video before the questionnaire filled in for the Strategic Consultancy, our task is to help people to live freely by giving them the opportunity to create an online activity capable of generating income, which is consistent with the current situation. That is, without changing your current lifestyle.

[EXPLAIN WHAT IT MEANS IN HIS SPECIFIC SITUATION - HE HAS TO UNDERSTAND AND BE CONFIDENT THAT HE DOESN'T HAVE TO CHANGE ANYTHING - EVEN IF HE TOLD YOU HE'S READY, HE'S NOT REALLY READY TO LEAVE THE COMFORT ZONE YET]

[EXPECT ME TO ASK YOU HOW ALL THIS WORKS]

Dreamworkers Team

Our program consists of an online training course that gives you the opportunity in 7 days to create and launch your own business.

You will receive video lessons every day that will guide you step by step in the realization of everything.

After 7 days, you will have lifetime access to the Member Area where there is all the advanced material and updates, and you can request access to a Private Facebook Group of Master Mind.

In this group there are only the people who have followed this path and the Customer Service Team.

This group is one of the most important elements because it takes advantage of the principle of "Learning By Doing", you learn by doing things every day and you are surrounded by successful people who share the same goals.

[NEVER GO INTO THE SPECIFICS OF THE PROGRAM AND NOT TALK ABOUT HOW IT IS STRUCTURED OR WHAT THE LESSONS ARE BECAUSE IT IS THE BEST WAY TO GREET YOUR POTENTIAL CUSTOMER - IF HE ASKS QUESTIONS

ALWAYS ANSWER IN GENERAL AND NOT TALK ABOUT PRICES - COMES THE MOMENT HE ASKS YOU HOW IT WORKS AND WHAT TO DO]

So ..., the program I told you about is called DREAMWORKERS ACCELERATOR and you can find it on the DreamWorkers Team's Facebook Page [I WANT YOU CAN ALSO CARRY ON THE PAGE IN WAY THAT I CAN SEE].

Its price is 1997€, but Matteo gave me the opportunity to reward people determined to achieve great goals and these people are those who act quickly.

That's why, now, I'm in a position to lower the price completely by transferring the best training course for free. You just need to work with us.

[NOW YOU JUST HAVE TO SHUT UP AND WAIT FOR HIM TO TALK - WHETHER HE ANSWERS POSITIVELY OR ASKS YOU HOW IT WORKS FOR THE PAYMENT]

You can sign up with me on the phone and pay by credit card or prepaid card.

[ANSWER WAIT - IF IT'S POSITIVE]

Is it a VISA, MASTERCARD or AMERICAN EXPRESS?

[TAKE THE DATA - 16 DIGITS, EXPIRATION AND CVV AND STOP SWEATING BECAUSE YOU'RE SELLING AN ASSET AND YOU SHOULD SWEAT LESS THAN THE SALESMAN WHO BUGGERS HIM 300€ FOR A PAIR OF SHOES WORTH 5€]

[AFTER YOU HAVE THE CARD DETAILS, ASK FOR CONFIRMATION OF THE OTHER DATA YOU NEED TO SIGN UP]

If you start with OBJECTIONS, manage them until you get to a YES or NO. If you close the Call with a maybe, the road to success is very but very but very but very but very far.]

OBJECTION: I HAVE NO MONEY

…how important is it for you to follow this program and achieve your goals?

[ANSWER ASPECTS]

The DREAMWORKERS ACCELERATOR comes for 1997€ and you know that right now I can give it to you for free.

Join ... with the smallest package comes $125, in euros less than 120€.

Are you really going to join this program?

Because if you don't, you can say it. There's nothing wrong with it.

[ANSWER YES, IF YES]

Well... how much time do you need to recover 120€?

[IF LESS THAN 3 DAYS OKAY, BLOCK THE OFFER, OTHERWISE BRING IT TO LESS THAN 3 DAYS]

Perfect, I'll keep you DREAMWORKERS ACCELERATOR free until ... I'll call you to finish.

If you don't answer me or fail by that date, you can join whenever you want and DREAMWORKERS ACCELERATOR will be back at 1997€.

[IT'S NOT A MARKETING STRATEGY - IF YOU DON'T STICK TO THE AGREEMENT, YOU PAY BECAUSE WE'RE WORKING HERE, NOT EATING PEANUTS]

OBJECTION: I HAVE TO THINK ABOUT IT

...how important is it for you to follow this program and achieve your goals?

[ANSWER ASPECTS]

Okay ..., what have I not dealt with during this call that does not allow you to understand whether to carry on this program with us or not?

[WAIT FOR AN ANSWER AND TRY TO UNDERSTAND THE REAL OBJECTION]

Are you really going to join this program?

Because if you don't, you can say it. There's nothing wrong with it.

[ANSWER YES, IF YES]

Well... how can I help you make a decision, positive or negative?

[TRY TO GET TO THE REAL PROBLEM, TAKE A DEADLINE AND CONTINUE WITH THE OFFER]

Perfect, I'll keep you DREAMWORKERS ACCELERATOR free until ... I'll call you to finish.

If you don't answer me or fail by that date, you can join whenever you want and DREAMWORKERS ACCELERATOR will be back at 1997€.

[IT'S NOT A MARKETING STRATEGY - IF YOU DON'T STICK TO THE AGREEMENT, YOU PAY BECAUSE WE'RE WORKING HERE, NOT EATING PEANUTS]

OBJECTION: I MUST ASK ...

...how important is it for you to follow this program and achieve your goals?

[ANSWER ASPECTS]

Okay ..., from what I understand you're really going to join this program but you need the consent of ... Is that it?

[ANSWER ASPECTS]

Perfect..., when do you think you're talking to...?

[YOU MUST HAVE A CERTAIN DATE]

Okay, I'll keep you DREAMWORKERS ACCELERATOR free until... I'll call you to finish.

If you don't answer me or fail by that date, you can join whenever you want and DREAMWORKERS ACCELERATOR will be back at 1997€.

[IT'S NOT A MARKETING STRATEGY - IF YOU DON'T STICK TO THE AGREEMENT, YOU PAY BECAUSE WE'RE WORKING HERE, NOT EATING PEANUTS]

OBJECTION: ANY OTHER

...how important is it for you to follow this program and achieve your goals?

[ANSWER ASPECTS]

[ASK QUESTIONS AND LEAD THE CONVERSATION UNTIL YOU FIGURE OUT THE REAL REASON]

Okay..., from what I understand you're really going to join this program but ... Is that it?

[ANSWER ASPECTS]

Perfect ...

[YOU MUST HAVE A CERTAIN DATE]

Okay, I'll keep you DREAMWORKERS ACCELERATOR free until... I'll call you to finish.

If you don't answer me or fail by that date, you can join whenever you want and DREAMWORKERS ACCELERATOR will be back at 1997€.

[IT'S NOT A MARKETING STRATEGY - IF YOU DON'T STICK TO THE AGREEMENT, YOU PAY BECAUSE WE'RE WORKING HERE, NOT EATING PEANUTS]

What you have just finished reading is the script that my team uses, at the time I wrote this book, and that's what has come to close even 8 contacts out of 10, after the person has gone through each phase of the entire system to 6 steps that I showed you.

It might seem like an out-of-the-ordinary result, but I assure you that you can get there with a lot of commitment and training because, after your marketing ecosystem has brought the contacts up to here, closing it will only be a matter of sensitivity and identifying its true point of pain.

Every person in the world earns money to spend and buys items every day to satisfy some cravings, so your only goal will be to understand exactly why your offer will be able to solve problems identified in calls or satisfy highlighted desires.

It doesn't matter what the price of your offer is, because the only thing that your potential customer is interested in is knowing that your product is suitable for his situation.

CHAPTER 7

SET A CORRECT FOLLOWUP

In this last chapter I enclose some followup emails that worked very well.

These are emails sent to people who have left the data on the opt-in page but have not requested advice.

In this first email I go to leverage on all the superficial people who leave the contact just to understand what you are talking about, but their interest is still low.

Hello ...,

Curiosity is a double-edged weapon that leads some to create an empire while others to fail miserably.

Over the years I have built various businesses in different niches of the market and it emerges that most people can not achieve what they want because it lets prevail the slight interest on the concentration of all the energies focused on a single point.

Dreamworkers Team

More than 50% of those who requested the video I sent yesterday did not look at it at all, as happens, after all, in all the other areas.

I know it sounds crazy, but it is.

The main hobby of these people is to leave fake names and invented email addresses to try to discover the secret, the magic trick that allows them to make money.

They forget, or pretend to forget, that in order to have a solid, profitable and scalable business, you need to get your ass kicked every day and have to improve and grow continuously.

In the video lesson that you received, and that you can watch by clicking below, I showed the 5 steps that give you the opportunity to achieve any turnover goal, but you have to make the decision to turn a simple desire into reality.

=> Links to watch the video and request advice

I'll see you soon,

Matthew

Network Marketing Online

SUBJECT: Curiosity kills you!

In this second email I leverage on all those people who think they don't have time, when in fact they just don't know how to handle it.

Hello ...,

I'm pretty sure you won't read this email all the way down to the end because part of your brain is already playing the usual "I don't have time, I have more to do" voice.

This voice is the one that divides successful people from those who exchange their time for money and are here to prove it to you.

Try to follow me for a moment... Most people earn an average salary that does not exceed 1500€ (if all goes well) working 8 hours a day, 5 days a week.

This means that if we multiply 40 hours per week by 4 weeks, we have 160 hours each paid €9.375.

So it's easy to come to the conclusion that half an hour of time for 95% of the population is worth 4.6875€.

Dreamworkers Team

If you've come this far and are still reading it means that your time will be worth a little more or you're determined for it to be worth it somehow in the future.

See ..., the video lesson that shows you the 5 steps to create from scratch an online activity that you should have seen (links to watch videos and request advice) lasts exactly that time and my statistics show that only 20% have completed the vision of the project, all the others have abandoned before or have not looked at it at all.

In that half hour it is explained in detail how we gave the opportunity to more than 700 people in the first months of activity to turn the experiences into a real profession that generated over $50,000.

Going back to doing the calculations, because everything else is simply poetry, $50,000 in 9 months means that we have maintained an average of $5,555.55 per month, devoting to this activity on average 4 hours a day.

In the first 9 months an hour of our time was evaluated, therefore, $69.44 which is 7 times the value of the time of 95%

of the population (without considering the difference that they work to go on vacation, while we go on vacation to work).

Then the question that arises is:

"Why doesn't 80% watch the presentation?"

For the same reason that in the next few years 66 million jobs will be burned because of robotics and digitization, while still that 95% continues to seek employment in the traditional sector.

In life there are people who take action and people who watch others take action, the decision on whose side to stand is up to you alone and only...

See you next time,

Matthew

P.S. Call to action with link to request advice.

SUBJECT: How much is half an hour of your time worth?

Dreamworkers Team

Here I emphasize, however, the fact that it is never a question of money, rather of lifestyle to achieve and mental tranquillity to have.

Hello ...,

I'm pretty sure you're not gonna read this email all the way down to the end

is already playing the usual "no time, no time, no time" vocal.

This voice is the one that divides successful people from those who exchange their time for money and are here to prove it to you.

Try to follow me for a moment... Most people earn an average salary that does not exceed 1500€ (if all goes well) working 8 hours a day, 5 days a week.

This means that if we multiply 40 hours per week by 4 weeks, we have 160 hours each paid €9.375.

So it's easy to come to the conclusion that half an hour of time for 95% of the population is worth 4.6875€.

Network Marketing Online

If you've come this far and are still reading it means that your time will be worth a little more or you're determined for it to be worth it somehow in the future.

See ..., the video lesson that shows you the 5 steps to create an online activity that you should have seen (links to watch videos and reserve the consulting) lasts exactly that time and my statistics show that only 20% have completed the vision of the project, all the others have abandoned before or have not looked at it at all.

In that half an hour it is explained in detail how we gave the opportunity to more than 700 people in the first months of activity to turn the experiences into a real profession that generated over $50,000.

Going back to doing the calculations, because everything else is simply poetry, $50,000 in 9 months means that we have maintained an average of $5,555.55 per month, devoting to this activity on average 4 hours a day.

In the first 9 months an hour of our time was evaluated, therefore, $69.44 which is 7 times the value of the time of 95%

of the population (without considering the difference that they work to go on vacation, while we go on vacation to work).

Then the question that arises is:

"Why doesn't 80% watch the presentation?"

For the same reason that in the next few years 66 million jobs will be burned because of robotics and digitization, while still that 95% continues to seek employment in the traditional sector.

In life there are people who take action and people who watch others take action, the decision on whose side to stand is up to you alone and only...

See you next time,

Matthew

P.S. Call to action with link to request advice.

SUBJECT: What is your lifestyle?

In the following, I leverage again on the chaos of a thousand things to do during the day that does not lead him to watch the video.

Hello ...,

Remember the first kiss?

You were on a log by the sea, in front of the most beautiful girl ever.

The wind was blowing, you were shaking and you didn't know if it was because of the strong emotion, you saw little hearts everywhere, you would have seen them even in the eyes of a lion.

You would have cloned that moment for a lifetime!

You were so immersed in the here and now that you had totally lost the conception of the past and the future.

The same conception you lost again... now!

You are so taken by everyday life, shopping, bills, children, that you can not take 30 minutes to fix the free Strategic Advice of the value of € 665 reserved for you.

Dreamworkers Team

You can't think where you'll be in 20 years...

I know it seems too far away and we've all fallen for it.

We are led to overestimate what we can do in 1 month and underestimate what we can do in 1 year!

I have transformed my life in a few months, imagine in years...

When I showed you the 5-step system that allowed me to achieve true freedom, you probably didn't pay the right attention or maybe you watched the video with superficiality, I can understand you.

Every day we celebrate important new qualifications achieved by the guys in our team, people who come to the same results, without any initial online skills.

They took my entire model and applied it without getting their hands on it. The first interested contacts arrived after a few hours and continued their lives without changing them in any way.

They will only be able to live on this new business in a few months and this is a fantastic result that fills me with joy.

Network Marketing Online

Reaching important goals is fantastic, seeing other people fulfill their desires is something else... an endless emotion.

I know very well that you can be so tired that you don't have the slightest desire to think or imagine what will come in your life in a few months... I think it deserves the best!

I'm sure you deserve to be on stage and be rewarded for reaching your goal, the one that will take you to live your life.

Each of us has a dream... a new car, a house, a different job, free time, etc...

This business is the means you need to get there, I got there and the guys from my team got there.

=> Link to request advice

Only you are missing... We're waiting for you!

A hug,

Matthew

OBJECT: Where will you be in 20 years' time?

Dreamworkers Team

In the following one I highlight that it is not a problem of technique, rather of mindset and that it will finally start successfully entering our team and taking the most advanced training program.

Hello ...,

The biggest lesson you have to take home from reading this email is that the main reason you are stuck in your current situation is not because of a lack of technique.

Over the years I've analyzed so many critical situations and trapped businesses and what I've learned is that you can have the best marketing system in the world, but if you don't have a winning mindset... you won't go anywhere!

There are exact patterns belonging to 1% of the population that turns everything it touches into gold, as there are deleterious patterns belonging to 99% of people who fail every day even before starting any stuff.

They fail:

- *In diets*

- *In sport*
- *In loving relationships*
- *In the business*
- *Anything else you can think of*

For this reason, the first video lesson of the advanced course DREAMWORKERS ACCELERATOR reserved for my team explains these patterns and how to install new paradigms that can lead us to achieve everything we want.

These are hours of training of a level never seen before in the Italian panorama!

The great thing is that you too can access this training, but first you have to ask for Strategic Advice because we need to understand exactly your situation and if we can help you achieve what is your main goal.

=> Link to reserve strategic advice

Remember that success begins the moment you make a decision!

I'll see you soon,

Dreamworkers Team

Matthew

As you can see these are very simple emails that, through different angles, go to push the contacts towards the advice or the video, if they have not watched it yet.

The easiest thing to do is to prepare an automation containing about twenty emails to be sent every 24 hours, trying during the process to remove any type of objection and showing, if you have, testimonials of success.

Then you can continue manually by sending the others with a slightly softer frequency or even every day if you have the opportunity.

I know you've been told that the opening rate of emails is getting lower and lower, and that's true, but the people who buy the most training programs are people who check their inbox and are used to receiving and sending emails.

CONCLUSION

If you've read so far, compared to your competitors, you're one step ahead and you'll not only be faster, but above all you'll build a solid, bomb-proof business.

Logically you can't try to start a scalable business having only read one book, so you'll at least have to delve into the whole technical part that will allow you to implement the whole system and start to deal with the first difficulties in the real world.

However, at this time, you know exactly what to do and how to do it and you know all the steps that will lead your potential customer to become a customer or agent.

Always remember that the most important part is to create something extremely easy, but at the same time complete, to be offered to the downline.

You have to give your boys the chance to devote themselves only to the lead generation without thinking about anything else and without having to train from scratch each new employee.

You'll have to remove every obstacle and every element that can lead them to abandon and try in every possible way to lead them to earn in a short time, to capture successful testimonies, to push more than anything else.

Remember that testimonials are never enough and the more money you see in your bank account, the better it will be.

Also, never neglect the sources of organic traffic and always use them before the paid ones because if you have in front of a boy who is not yet able, you risk to make him leave immediately.

Your goal is to keep as much time as possible for the active agents and to do this they have to live a non-traumatic and gradual path.

If their sales system is not solid yet, you cannot bring paid traffic into the optin page because they will not be able to convert it and will throw money out of the window.

Also check the system conversion rate and the ROI of each campaign, you need to understand exactly how much you are investing and how much you are going back.

This is one of the biggest obstacles that does not lead networkers to scale a network marketing business, because many times the conversion rates are excellent, but the ROI is negative.

It means that your lead generation is losing money and, if you don't have a sales system that will lead to rapid duplication, it's unlikely to be sustainable in the long run.

For this reason, I have decided to dedicate another book, which I will write shortly, entirely on this subject.

By now the number of advertisers on Facebook is growing out of all proportion and contacts are becoming more and more expensive, so there is no margin for error like in the past when contacts were acquired for fifty cents.

It brings people to work in an organic way, creating an ad hoc system that can adapt to their daily lives, and always push on the product because, regardless of economic results, the basis is a quality product or service that must be used.

Creating a philosophy that keeps people inside even without earning money is important because, in the worst case, you will have satisfied consumers of the product and happy to order and recommend it.

This part is often forgotten by the most aggressive networkers, oriented only and exclusively to business and I am definitely one of them, but the strongest and most solid networks are always those that consume the product and there is no history or discussion.

In this book you have found all the tools you need to be successful, now you just have to go out there, find someone who is in target and communicate your offer correctly.

STRATEGIC PS

THE REAL PROBLEM WITH THE FUNNELS

The people you already have on your team…

If you already have a large team with people who are unlikely to be able to use an advanced system, such as the one I just showed you, you will find the solution below.

I had the same problem because I had many people in my downline who have always worked with list names and traditional systems and who continue inexorably to recruit in this way.

Obviously, rather than losing them, it is better to create something that can help them to work in a slightly more professional way.

So I created two landing pages, in which I inserted the video presentation of the opportunity and the video presentation of the 5-phase system, adding photos and testimonials.

This prevents them from bringing traffic to company pages or simply working with videos uploaded to YouTube.

Working like this, you have the possibility through the Facebook monitoring pixel to follow these people with specific followups that, many times, your downline will not do.

In other words, avoid losing traffic and keep control over all the people who interact with your pages.

In addition, I have included a section within the members area to which all new appointees have access, where I show exactly how to work in the traditional way using these tools, so as to reassure everyone and not risk losing those who want to work the old way.

... and the high number of advertisers...

In recent years many "gurus" in network marketing have positioned themselves for difference by aggressively disqualifying all those who used the list names.

Initially they got a lot of visibility because there was still little offer on Social Media and advertising costs were still very low. Let's say it was enough to be a minimum capable of putting two pages in a row and some results arrived.

With the passing of time and with the increase in the number of advertisers, it has become increasingly difficult to set up a profitable advertising campaign, as on the one hand only increased advertising costs and on the other hand the competition has become increasingly aggressive.

To be successful it was no longer enough to launch a recruitment funnel from a Facebook page opened a few days ago, containing only a few images, rather there was a need to differentiate and show why the potential customer should choose you instead of another.

Then the positioning of the "gurus" who go from discrediting the list of names to attacking the other trainers starts to change, saying that that specific type of funnel did not work because the other one brought interesting results.

And here begins the real chaos that leads networkers to no longer understand what to do and what funnels to use, because each proposes a different one and, even, there are totally different funnels to promote products or opportunities of the same company.

The truth is that many of these "gurus" simply earn from the training courses without having really tested the funnel they propose, otherwise they would know the real problems that lie behind it.

The main problem, at the time I wrote this book, is not on which funnel to use, although surely structuring one correctly is important.

You have a perfect understanding of how to create it at this point in the book, so you don't have any problems with that.

The real obstacle is to win the war of the advertising cost that rises more and more on Social Media and understand how to promote the opportunity without annihilating your current account.

Underneath I drop random numbers to make you understand exactly what I'm talking about...

100 X 0,30 = 30€

30€ / 15 lead = 2€

30€ / 7 = 4,29€

If we had used this funnel when advertising costs were low and competition less aggressive, considering a cost per lead of 30 cents, we would have spent 2€ for each lead arrived in strategic consulting and 4.29€ for each recruiter, if the conversion rate had been about 50%.

If even one person had been incompetent and had launched any totally wrong funnel and had converted even just 1% into a commissioner, he would have spent €30 on a commissioner and most likely would have regained this amount from selling the product or business opportunity.

Today, unfortunately or fortunately, this is no longer the case and there is no more room for those who improvise by launching some campaign sponsored to the right or left without meaning.

Let's change some numbers...

100 X 2,00 = 200€

200€ / 15 lead = 13,33€

200€ / 7 = 28,57€

Are you starting to feel the pain?

You pay 100 lead 200€, you can take home 15 strategic advice at 13,33€ and if you close 7 you have a cost per person of 28,57€.

I said before "luckily" because in this new condition the amateur networker comes home and stops improvising a business, leaving room for professionals.

This new situation is a problem for all networkers, because at most you can build a team in frontend with a ROI that is equal to zero.

As soon as the system starts to creak a little, you go immediately in negative and you find yourself building a team having to invest money that "maybe" will come back.

And here someone could tell me "yes ok you're right, but I'm building a team that works and that generates other commissions, besides the direct ones".

This statement, theoretically, is not wrong because you have a well formed downline that could develop in depth and lead you to earn much more than what you invest.

The problem is that we have to consider two elements of fundamental importance:

1. Duplicable system.
2. Incubation period.

The duplicable system is the first thing you must have to make sure that the accounts can return and you can continue to make lead generation even slightly in negative.

We have seen in this book how to build it and we have also seen a soft variant for all people who want to continue to work organically using the traditional method.

The incubation period is the second thing to consider, much more important than the first, that every networker forgets, especially the fake gurus who have never tested the systems they teach.

You should know that there are three stages in marketing:

1. Contact generation.
2. Nurturing.
3. Sale.

There is an initial moment when you start talking about your product or opportunity by trying to generate the first contacts, there is a second phase in which you educate them and a third phase in which you turn them into customers or agents.

It is not certain that when you launch an advertisement the person who sees it is immediately ready to give you their contact, could leave it to you even after a seventh, a month or, even as often happens, three or four months.

There are people watching you for six months before they leave you their contact, because they want to see if you stay on the market, how you move, what you do, if they can trust you and if your product could be right for them.

During this period, when you have not acquired their contact yet, you still have to educate them through the various channels, which can be Facebook pages, Instagram profiles, Blogs, videos on YouTube and so on.

If you do what all those who educate contacts do only after they get the email, you can be sure that what they need to observe you for six months you will definitely lose.

You must have, therefore, a marketing ecosystem that educates both those who do not leave the contact and those who have already left and is slowly moving towards the purchase of your product or your opportunity.

All this is called the "incubation period" and is the real drama of networkers who start to develop their online business.

It is a real drama because you may have a stellar conversion rate, above the market average, but a long incubation period that leads you to have to invest money for months having suffered back a few agents.

To this you will have to add the second incubation period between the moment when a contact becomes in charge and the moment when the person in charge starts recruiting the first people.

The more complex your training system is, the longer the second incubation period of a person in charge will be.

Now, I know very well that you might be afraid to read all this, but this is real and the more we go forward the more difficult it will be because the advertising costs will increase and you will no longer have the opportunity to depend on a single platform.

Network Marketing Online

In such a situation, you either have a budget to invest or you need to have a second system that can cover your advertising costs, allowing you to make free lead generation and build lists in target of potential agents.

This will be the subject of the next book I will write, and you can buy it to understand exactly how to implement a system capable of recruiting covering advertising costs.

There are several ways to do this and you can start from the product or the business opportunity, training first the people we will recruit later, as I do with this funnel -> *http://bit.ly/dreamworkersreclutator*).

In this case, I offer networkers the basic version of my advanced program that will give them the opportunity to learn how to do network marketing in a sustainable and scalable way, then they can use it for their project or start the business with me and take the rest of the advanced program for free.

It's a very smart strategy, because it shortens the second incubation period, having already trained the people in charge of the activities with you, and it creates a base of people in target on which to set up retargeting campaigns.

In my case, there were also a lot of satisfied customers of other networks because they received for the first time a system actually used and explained through the screen sharing, showing everything we do every day.

It is true that giving your system to anyone is not really the best, but it gives you a way to strengthen your brand and be perceived more and more as an authority within this market and, if you work well, people will always choose you.

The market is tired of receiving copy and paste funnels, and hours of theory. People want to see something that worked and want to know how to use it to solve their problems.

Above all you have to remember that 96% of networkers do not earn a single euro cent throughout their careers, which means that almost all those who buy in your system have no results and do not know where to bump their heads.

If you offer them the chance to earn money and turn network marketing into a profitable business, I can assure you that they will stay with you because their goal is not to sell one product rather than the other, but to earn and live a relaxed life.

As I told you earlier, the more problems you can solve, the more people you can solve these problems to, the better your business results will be.

Doing this is certainly not easy, but it gives you the opportunity to differentiate yourself totally from your competitors and have an important advantage.

You must try in every possible way to create something that cannot be duplicated, that goes beyond simple video lessons and that goes beyond the simple system.

If you create a community in which your distributors can grow, learning every day from others who had the same difficulties and have overcome them, you have built the foundations for the greatest legacy that can come to you in the future.

Starting a network marketing business online is far from easy because, in most cases, we are dealing with companies that pay us low commissions and we can not margine immediately, but at the same time is the fastest way to create a large network that extends internationally.

Every great difficulty carries with it the seed of an equivalent or even greater advantage that, if we know how to grasp, allows us to live a life as we have always wanted it.

The biggest lesson you can learn from this and every other book I've written is that network marketing, like any self-respecting real business, needs huge investments in time and money.

If you consider that a person who starts a restaurant needs years before he returns from the investment and starts earning money, you immediately realize the enormous advantage that you have in carrying out a network marketing activity.

In this business we have, however, the opportunity to earn immediately and this gives us the opportunity to earn years compared to any other traditional business, so investing a few thousand euros to create a solid foundation is not so wrong.

The secret is to create the right expectations and work only and exclusively with people who have the desire to achieve important results, even better if these people have the economic peace to be able to cope with any obstacle along the way.

It tries in every possible way to keep away the opportunities seeker and all those who try to achieve results in a few weeks, because they will ruin all your work, will complain continuously and will be the first to leave negative feedback on your work and the business opportunity that you are offering.

SPECIAL OFFER

As a special thank you for purchasing this book, I have prepared an exclusive gift for you.

Now you can join the DreamWorkers Team and receive the most advanced program in Italy on Network Marketing, **DREAMWORKERS ACCELERATOR**, for free instead of 1.997€.

Click on the following link to watch our presentation and reserve a 30-minute strategic consultancy with one of our coaches.

=> https://bit.ly/dwtexpansion <=

Follow us on our Facebook Page:

=> https://www.facebook.com/dreamworkersteam/

Printed in Poland
by Amazon Fulfillment
Poland Sp. z o.o., Wrocław

71106792R00107